SCIENTIFIC INVENTORY CONTROL

OPERATIONAL RESEARCH SERIES

General Editor
K. B. Haley, Ph.D
Professor of Operational Research in Engineering
  Production — The University of Birmingham

This series of books on Operational Research covers in depth practical considerations of the most important techniques. Too often in the past texts have appeared which are largely theoretical in content. The aim of this series is to present the material in a form which can be readily used by practitioners. Each book will be written by an expert in the practical and theoretical aspects of his subject. A mathematical knowledge which would be obtained by a good school leaver is assumed and any more advanced methods that may be required will be developed. Currently in preparation are books in the fields of inventory, simulation, queueing, graphs and networks, replacement and dynamic programming, and it is planned to extend the series into a number of other fields including mathematical programming. The series will be equally suited for individual reading or for use as text books on organised courses.

Scientific
inventory control

C. D. LEWIS, PH.D., C. ENG., M.I.E.E., M.I. PROD. E.

AMERICAN ELSEVIER PUBLISHING COMPANY, INC.
NEW YORK

658.787
L 673

Published in the United States by
American Elsevier Publishing Company, Inc.
52 Vanderbilt Avenue, New York, NY 10017

First Published in England, 1970 by

Butterworth & Co (Publishers) Ltd

88 Kingsway London WC2B 6AB

© C. D. Lewis, 1970

Printed in Hungary

Contents

Preface

Management is becoming increasingly aware that the overall efficiency of company's operation is directly related to inventory situation existing within the company. Thus, there has been an increasing requirement for a knowledge of the mathematical theory which can be used to analyse and control stocks. Unfortunately, inventory control is a topic which workers in the field of operational research (or management science) have found mathematically interesting and thus a great deal of complex work on inventory control has appeared in the literature. As a result it is often said of inventory control that theory is years ahead of practice, and that the real need currently is to ensure that a much greater proportion of this mathematical knowledge is interpreted into practice. Against this argument, however, is the fact that any analysis of a practical inventory situation is bound to be reasonably mathematically complicated. Simple models which assume constant demand and instantaneous delivery of replenishment orders are all very well for explaining principles but rarely if ever occur.

This book is an attempt to 'bridge the gap' between, on the one hand the ultra-simple inventory models having little relevance in the practical situation and on the other, the sophisticated mathematical theory concerned with inventory control currently appearing in the literature. Thus, probabilistic inventory models are considered throughout but an attempt has been made to involve only that mathematical and statistical theory which is absolutely essential. Each chapter has been terminated with a set of questions with answers so that the reader may practice on the material presented.

Because it is hoped that to some extent this book should be used as a reference after an initial reading, a complete Glossary and collection of equations are provided in the Appendices. Thus when familiarity with the work presented in each chapter has been established, reference need be made only to these Appendices.

Acknowledgments

I wish to express my appreciation to both Bob Woodman and Bernard Tate, Operational Research Managers at the British Shoe Corporation and International Printers Limited respectively, for checking through the manuscript of this book and for their many helpful suggestions during its preparation.

I would like to thank Bernard Tate yet again for permission to use his joint re-order level and replenishment order quantity model described in Chapter 3, and also John Murdoch (Senior Lecturer at the College of Aeronautics, Cranfield) for permission to use his work on coverage analysis which forms the basis of Chapter 8.

Finally, thanks are due to my colleague Brian Haley, editor of the series, who suggested I write this book and who made many helpful suggestions for its content, and to Bobbie Kerton for having typed the manuscript with so few errors.

CHAPTER 1

Introduction to Inventory Control

Inventory control is the science-based art of controlling the amount of stock held, in various forms, within a business to meet economically the demands placed upon that business.

Such a business can vary from the international company operating throughout the world and subjected to demands in both imports and exports, to the small specialist firm supplying a larger organisation. Inventory control is usually associated with industry, but many inventory control problems do occur in other organisations such as the armed services, transport undertakings, hospitals, etc.

Stocks held by a business can occur in many forms. One usually thinks only in terms of either finished product stocks (that is the saleable items waiting for despatch) or the raw material stocks held in stores which are used to make up the finished product. However, in between these two types are all the in-process stocks which occur naturally as part of the production process. Even the machinery used for the latter could be regarded as stocks of production capacity subjected to a demand of utilisation time.

REASONS FOR HOLDING STOCK

In an ideal world, where the demand upon a business is known exactly and well in advance and where suppliers keep to their due dates, there would be little need to hold any form of inventory other than a limited amount of in-process stocks caused as a by-product of the manufacturing process. Such a problem would be one only of scheduling, which although possibly complicated, would be completely deterministic because all the problem parameters would be exactly defined.

In practice however, demand is not known in advance and suppliers will often be late—or even early—in delivering. In this imperfect but practical situation, stocks can act as a buffer between the vagaries of supply and demand.

The principal reasons for holding stock are:

(*a*) To act as an insurance against higher-than-average demand. This helps to ensure that customer demand will more often than not be met, resulting in satisfied customers and, hence, continued demand

(*b*) To act as an insurance against longer-than-average supplier delivery times, this usually being termed in inventory control as the 'leadtime'. Customers demanding their usual quota of goods are unlikely to be impressed by the excuse that one's supplies are late, especially if they can obtain the same goods elsewhere

(*c*) To take advantage of quantity discounts. It may be advantageous to purchase more supplies than are immediately required, and to incur the slightly higher holding and storage costs, if these increases in costs are more than offset by the reduction in an item's unit cost as a result of the large quantity purchase

(*d*) To take advantage of seasonal and other price fluctuations. The householder in Britain who buys coal during the summer rightly assumes that the consequent saving in material costs more than outweighs the negligible increased storage and investment costs. For the coal supplier, however, this seasonal price reduction stimulates demand in an otherwise slack period and so reduces production costs by levelling demand over the year

(e) To minimise delay in production caused by a lack of parts. With products comprising many components and subassemblies, it is administratively nearly impossible to ensure that one of each of all these parts arrive simultaneously at a final assembly point. In this situation, stocks of components and subassemblies at assembly points act as a buffer within the production system to absorb the demand that the system exerts on itself.

The aim of an inventory control system is to maintain the quantities of stocks held by a business at a level which optimises some management criteria such as minimising the costs incurred by the whole business enterprise as a result of holding stocks, maximising the business's profits or providing a stated minimum customer service. There are obviously disadvantages in holding either too much stock or too little and some of these are indicated below.

DISADVANTAGES OF LOW STOCK LEVELS

(a) Customer demand can often not be satisfied. This can lead to an immediate loss of business, also to a loss of future business through customer dissatisfaction

(b) Because of (a), costly emergency procedures such as special production runs and upset schedules are often resorted to in an attempt to maintain customer goodwill

(c) To maintain a reasonable service it will be necessary (on average) to place replenishment orders more frequently than in the situation where higher stock levels are kept. Thus higher replenishment ordering costs are incurred.

DISADVANTAGES OF HIGH STOCK LEVELS

(a) Storage costs incurred are very high. These costs not only cover buildings, labour, heating, etc., but must also allow for deterioration and spoilage

(*b*) The increased loss on capital invested in stocks can become prohibitive. One large British company maintains that the interest lost on money invested in stocks can boost the holding cost of an item up to a value of about 20 per cent of the material and labour, or work's prime cost. Working on an assumed rate of 21·6 per cent this can be simply evaluated as 1d/£/week. Although this figure may appear too simple a generalisation of the real situation, it does provide a guide which can be easily interpreted by employees; that is, for every £'s worth of material lying about for a week a holding cost to the firm of 1d is incurred (Note: 1p = 2·4d).

(*c*) Where the stored product becomes obsolete, a large stockholding of that item could, in the worst situation, represent a large capital investment in an unsaleable product whose cash value is only that of scrap

(*d*) A high capital investment in stocks necessarily means that there is less money available within the business for other requirements such as the enlargement and improvement of existing production facilities or the introduction of new products

(*e*) When a high stock level of a raw material is held, a sudden drop in the going market price of that material represents a cash loss to the business for having bought at the higher price previously existing. (However, should the going market price of the material go up, a cash benefit is derived.) Although it is virtually impossible to predict market changes should they exist, it would appear sensible to hold higher stocks in a period of general inflation than in a period of deflation.

A company's stockholding policy is implemented by a series of rules which determine how and when certain decisions concerning the holding of stocks should be made. This series of rules is known as an 'inventory policy'.

There are two basic types of inventory policy. That in which decisions concerning replenishment are based on the level of inventory held is known as 're-order level' policy, and that in which such decisions are made on a time basis is known as 're-order cycle' policy. Within these two categories there are several variants and those which are most used in practice are described below.

INVENTORY POLICIES

The Re-order Level Policy (often implemented as the two-bin system)

In this inventory policy, an order for replenishment is placed when the stock on-hand (which not only includes the current stock actually held but also any outstanding replenishment orders) equals or falls below a fixed value M known as the re-order level. In this policy, therefore, the amount of inventory held must be reviewed continuously.

When a replenishment order is placed within a re-order level policy, it is for a fixed quantity. A typical example of inventory balances for

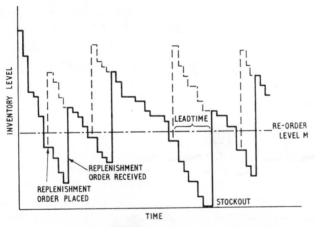

Fig. 1.1. Typical stock balances for a re-order level policy

a re-order level policy is shown in Fig. 1.1. The solid line in this diagram represents the actual inventory held in the practical situation where a finite leadtime exists; the leadtime being defined as the time delay between the placing of a replenishment order and its subsequent receipt. The broken line indicates the inventory that would be held in the ideal situation if no leadtime existed, that is, if replenishment orders were fulfilled immediately. This broken line then represents the stock on-hand.

The most common practical implementation of the re-order level policy is as the two-bin system. Here, two bins of the stocked item are kept and a replenishment order is placed when the first bin becomes empty; stock is withdrawn from the second bin until the replenishment order is received. Thus, the amount of stock held in the second bin represents the size of the re-order level. In practice, of course, it is not always necessary to have two separate bins to operate this system; for instance a single bin with a dividing layer or partition serves exactly the same purpose. This single-bin adaption of the method cannot, however, be used for items that deteriorate or for those which for some reason must be controlled with a 'first in–first out' policy unless removal is possible from the bottom of the container.

The single- or two-bin system operates most successfully with physically small items such as nuts, bolts, washers, etc. The system obviously becomes impracticable when considering large items such as castings, subassemblies, etc., as these cannot be so arranged that when the number remaining reaches a specified amount this is immediately apparent.

The Re-order Level Policy with Periodic Reviews

As has been mentioned earlier, for a re-order level policy to be operated successfully the amount of stock on-hand must be checked continuously. While this is convenient when operating a single- or two-bin system, it is often not possible when operating a re-order level policy in which paper records of the stock on-hand are kept and where these records are updated only at certain intervals of time. This is generally the situation with all but the smallest items; records being kept of stock items which can be located on several different shelves or even in different locations within a store. Here it is possible to operate a re-order level inventory policy with periodic reviews, typical

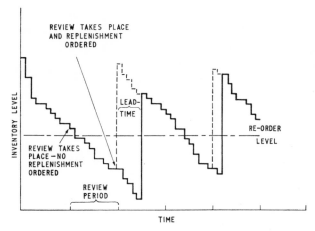

Fig. 1.2. Typical stock balances for a re-order level policy with periodic reviews

stock balances for which are shown in Fig. 1.2. The rules governing this policy are that at each review, only if the stock on-hand lies below or at the re-order level should an order for replenishment be placed. When a replenishment order is placed it is for a fixed quantity as in the true re-order level policy.

The Re-order Cycle Policy

In this inventory policy the stock on-hand is reviewed periodically and a replenishment order placed at every review. However, unlike those policies previously described, when a replenishment order is placed for this policy, its size is variable. This variable replenishment quantity is calculated as that amount of stock which, if there were no leadtime, would bring the stock on-hand up to some fixed level S. Thus, the size of the replenishment order is equal to S less the inventory on-hand, and can be different at every review. This policy ensures that when the level of stock on-hand is high at review, a smaller sized replenishment order is placed than when it is low. This can be quite clearly seen in Fig. 1.3. which shows a typical stock situation when operating a re-order cycle policy.

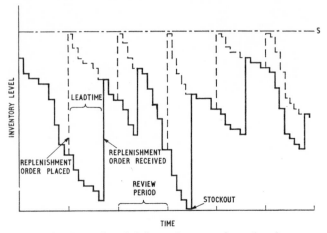

Fig. 1.3. Typical stock balances for a re-order cycle policy

The (s, S) Policy

The (s, S) policy is again a policy in which the stock on-hand is reviewed periodically. The rules governing the operation of this policy are that if at review the stock on-hand is at or below a level s a replenishment order is placed; if the stock on-hand is above s no replenishment order is placed. This criterion of when to place an order is exactly the same as for the re-order level policy with periodic reviews, with s now replacing M. However, in the (s, S) policy the size of the replenishment order placed is calculated on the same basis as for the re-order cycle policy (i.e. as S less the stock on-hand). The name (s, S) is given to this policy because S represents the fixed inventory level from which the replenishment order sizes are calculated, and s the level to which the stock on-hand must have fallen at review for a further replenishment order to be placed. Fig. 1.4 indicates a typical inventory balance situation for an (s, S) policy, and points in time where a review took place, but because the inventory on-hand was above s no further replenishment order was placed, are indicated.

The (s, S) policy and the re-order level policy with periodic reviews are exactly similar in their method of assessing when a replenishment order is to be placed; but it is the different methods by which the size of the replenishment order quantity is calculated that distinguish the two. By adjustment of their control parameters, both policies can be made to exhibit characteristics of either the re-order level or re-order cycle policy.

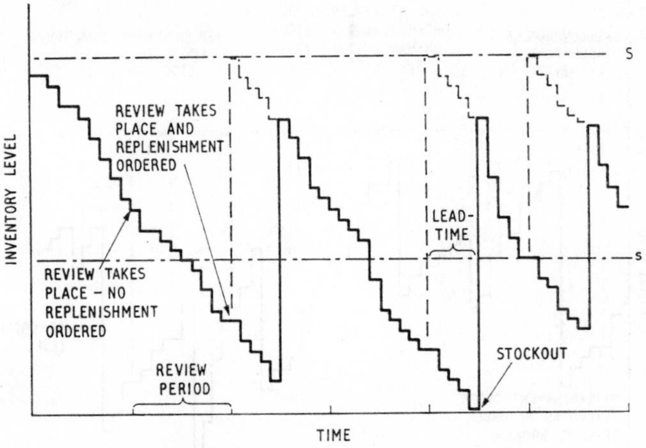

Fig. 1.4. Typical stock balances for an (s, S) policy

The Combined Re-order Level and Re-order Cycle Policy

Although both the re-order level policy with periodic reviews and the (s, S) policy are variants of the two basic policies (i.e. the re-order level policy and the re-order cycle policy) a possible inventory policy could just combine the two. A typical inventory balance situation for such a combined policy is shown in Fig. 1.5. In this policy, replenishment orders are placed periodically not only when the stock on-hand is reviewed but also at times between reviews should the stock on-hand fall below the re-order level. For this policy, because some replenishment orders are placed on a stock on-hand basis as well as periodically, the stock on-hand must be monitored continuously unless a two-bin type of system can be operated. A true combination of the re-order level and re-order cycle policies would require that the size of those replenishment orders placed when the re-order level was broken be fixed, but those placed at review be variable (i.e. calculated as a level S less the stock on-hand). In practice, however, when this type of policy is used the size of the replenishment order is calcu-

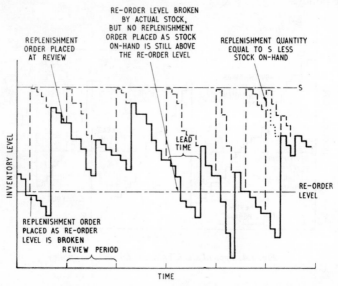

Fig. 1.5. Typical stock balances for a combined re-order level and re-order cycle policy

lated as S minus the stock on-hand irrespective of the criteria on which the placing of that order was made.

BACKORDERING

With all the inventory policies described, should a stockout occur (i.e. the stock level fall to zero), one is left with a choice of whether to backorder or not.

When backordering is not permitted, for the final demand order which reduces the stock held to zero, that stock which is available is sent in part fulfillment of the order and the customer is either advised to purchase the balance elsewhere or is notified when further stocks are available. In this situation, when a stockout does occur the stock level remains at zero until replenishment arrives, at which time the full value of the replenishment order is added to the inventory held. This procedure can be seen in Fig. 1.6a where, at the first stockout, a replenishment order for 400 units raises the inventory level to 400.

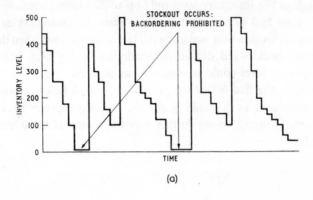

(a)

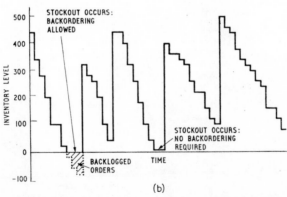

(b)

Fig. 1.6. Inventory balances with backordering (a) prohibited (b) permitted

When backordering is permitted, for the final demand order which reduces the stock held to zero, that stock which is available is sent in part fulfillment of this final order and the balance is promised for delivery as soon as further stocks are available. Further demand orders which arrive before the replenishment order are similarly committed for immediate delivery on replenishment and thus a backlog of orders is built up. This process is known as 'backordering' and has the effect of reducing the level of inventory held immediately after replenishment. This can be seen in Fig. 1.6b where after the first situation at which a stockout occurs, a replenishment order for 400 units brings the inventory level only up to 320 units: because orders for 80 units had previously been committed to customers as backordering in this situation was allowed. It is apparent that when demand orders are backlogged due to backordering having been permitted, the inventory level could be regarded as negative.

Although the five inventory policies described here do not cover every type used in controlling stocks, they do represent the basic types, others usually being further sophistications of these five basic methods.

CHAPTER 2

Analysis of Customer Demand: Short-term Forecasting Techniques

Before one can attempt to implement an effective inventory control system, one must analyse the customer demand to which the business's inventory will be subjected. It is usual when analysing this demand to measure the demand per unit time rather than to investigate the actual size of individual orders. This is because all inventory policies are dependent on time, either in the form of review periods or lead-time durations. The unit of time used may vary considerably from perhaps a year for slow moving items such as spare parts for capital equipment to a day for fast moving stock items such as perishables.

When analysing the customer demand per unit time, three main factors should be known. The first is the 'average' (or mean) demand per unit time. An estimate of the mean demand per unit time will give an indication of what demand would be expected in a typical time period. It must be realised that such a mean value can only be calculated from past data, and to use such a value to predict what will happen in the future implies that one assumes that what has happened in the past will necessarily happen again and, of course, this is rarely so. The value of the mean gives only an indication of what demand per unit time should occur in a typical time period. There are many

13

ways of estimating the mean value of the demand per unit time and several of these are explained later in this chapter.

The second parameter required in analysing customer demand per unit time is the 'standard deviation' which gives an indication of how the actual demand per unit time fluctuates about the mean value already described. With a measure of the standard deviation available, one can begin to estimate the probability that the demand per unit time will exceed a specified value during a certain time period with a known degree of confidence.

Although the mean and standard deviation give an indication of the central tendency of the value of demand per unit time and the spread of values about that central figure respectively, for any statistical analysis of demand data to be complete it is necessary to know from what type of 'probability distribution' the data on demand orders may be drawn. Rarely if ever will the pattern of demand have an exact mathematical probability distribution, but for practical purposes the pattern of demand may come very close to a particular distribution. In this chapter three of the most commonly used mathematical probability distributions are described, and the situations in which the demand data frequency distribution is likely to be very similar to them are also detailed.

ESTIMATING THE MEAN DEMAND PER UNIT TIME

There are many methods of 'forecasting' what the average value of demand will be in the future. This book will deal with the simpler methods used and readers interested in more sophisticated techniques are referred to the list of references provided at the end of the chapter.

When estimating the mean value of demand per unit time, one of the first assumptions that must be made is whether or not the demand data are drawn from a *stationary* distribution. This is a distribution in which it is assumed that the mean value remains constant although individual values may well vary considerably. This assumption is not valid in the situation of a rapidly expanding market; and in that situation one has not only to estimate the mean value but also attempt to measure the rate of growth of that mean value with time.

If one can assume that the demand data are drawn from a stationary demand distribution, then any estimate made of the mean value at the present time will be the best estimate of that mean for all time. This does not imply, however, that when a further piece of demand data is available that one cannot readjust the value of that forecast of the mean in the light of the more recent data received. It must be realised that demand data are drawn from a distribution which is never known exactly and, therefore, estimates of what a particular demand distribution is are indeed only estimates of what one hopes to be the general situation.

MOVING AVERAGE

This is the simplest form of an estimate for the mean value of a stationary demand process. The moving average is calculated very simply by dividing the sum of the demand in the last n time periods (say the last six months) by n (i.e. 6). Although very simple to calculate, the moving average has two main disadvantages, namely:

(*a*) It is necessary to store demand data for the last $n-1$ time periods in order to calculate a fresh forecast

(*b*) When beginning the calculation of a moving average from demand data, because for the previous $n-1$ periods must be available, no true forecast can be made until at least n periods have passed. This snag can be overcome to a certain extent by using an 'initialised moving average'.

An initialised moving average is calculated by dividing the sum of the data so far available by the number of periods from which that data is drawn until $n-1$ periods have passed; then from the nth period onwards the true moving average can be calculated. As an example of this procedure; at the first time period the forecast of the mean value for the second time period would be the same as that value of the demand which occurred in the first period. However, in the second period the forecast for the third period would be the sum of the demand values in the first two months divided by two. The forecasting process would then continue in such a manner until (assuming a six period moving average were being considered) values of demand for six periods were available. From then onwards the sum of the last six period's demand values would be calculated by adding the most recent period's value to the total and subtracting the value of demand which occurred in the period now seven periods old. This sum divided by 6 would then form a true six period moving average.

Whichever of the two methods described is used, at the beginning of a forecasting process it is always necessary to make an initial guess at what the average might be. Without such a guess the assumption is that the mean value is zero, and such a ridiculous assumption will generally produce large forecasting errors over the first few periods.

Table 2.1 shows various types of six month moving average calculated from one year's monthly demand data. It should be noted that for the true (i.e. the uninitialised) moving average, the initial estimate will remain the forecast of the average demand for the first n (in this case six) months.

A measure often used to indicate whether one method of forecasting is better than another is based on the sum of the squared forecasting errors which is one way of ensuring that *all* errors make a contribution to the comparison. Using this criterion, it can be seen that the true moving average with no initial estimate is significantly worse than the other three methods, as would be expected. Of the other three forecasting methods, the initialising moving average with an initial estimate produces the lowest squared errors sum, the true moving average with an initial estimate is next best, and the initialised moving average with no initial estimate is the worst of these three. Although the accuracies of forecasts based on the various types of moving average described need not necessarily occur ranked in this order, it can be generally stated that any type of moving average with an initial estimate will produce less forecasting errors than one without, and that when beginning a forecasting system based on the moving average principle an initialised moving average will produce less forecasting errors over the first $n-1$ periods than a true moving average

Table 2.1. COMPARISON OF DIFFERENT TYPES OF SIX MONTH MOVING AVERAGE

Monthly demand	Jan	Feb	Mar	Apr	May	Jun	Jul	Aug	Sep	Oct	Nov	Dec	Sum of squared forecasting errors
	48	60	50	72	80	60	66	72	80	61	65	75	
True six month moving average with no initial estimate*	0	0	0	0	0	0	62	65	66	67	64	64	24 007
True six month moving average with an initial estimate of 50*	50	50	50	50	50	50	62	65	66	67	64	64	3 005
Initialised six month moving average with no initial estimate*	0	48	54	53	57	62	62†	65	66	67	64	64	3 777
Initialised six month moving average with an initial estimate of 50*	50	48	54	53	57	62	62†	65	66	67	64	64	1 058

* Note: The values calculated are shown in the month for which the forecast was intended although in fact this value was calculated in the previous month. For example for the initialised six month moving average the value calculated in February as (48+60)/2 = 54, is entered for the month of March as this was the month for which the forecast of 54 was attempting to predict what the demand would be. The demand for this month was in fact 50, thus producing a forecasting error of 4
† End of initialising period, the first true six month average formed

with a single estimate whose value acts as the forecast over the whole of this time. After the initialising period all moving averages are calculated on exactly the same basis and, therefore, all produce the same forecast.

EXPONENTIALLY WEIGHTED AVERAGE

Many of the disadvantages of the moving average can be overcome by using a form known as the 'exponentially weighted average'. In the sense in which it is used here, *weighting* means the proportion of the eventual value of the average being formed that each individual piece of data contributes. Referring back to the six period moving average, it is evident that each piece of data contributes 1/6th of its value to the eventual value of the moving average. As there are six pieces of data it is also evident that the sum of the weights is one (i.e. $6 \times 1/6 = 1$), and this is the definition of a true average; namely that the sum of the weights must be unity.

Looking now at the formation of an average as the sum of weighted data, it is apparent that the moving average is a rather crude form. Data in the last n periods are weighted equally by $1/n$ and data older than this are ignored, i.e. given zero weighting. Perhaps a much more sensible method of forming an average would be to have the weightings gradually becoming smaller as the data became older and this would then overcome the sudden rejection of information of more than n periods old, as necessarily happens with the moving average.

A series whose values become progressively smaller and whose sum to infinity is equal to one, is the exponential series, defined as

$$\alpha + \alpha(1-\alpha) + \alpha(1-\alpha)^2 + \ldots = 1 \qquad (2.1)$$

where α is a constant between 0 and 1

It can be shown that the exponentially weighted average, that is, an average whose data weighting decreases exponentially with time, is given by the equation

$$u_t = \alpha y_t + (1-\alpha)u_{t-1} \qquad (2.2)$$

where, u_t is the exponentially weighted average calculated in the present period

      u_{t-1} is the exponentially weighted average calculated in the immediate past period

      y_t is the value of the demand per unit time which has occurred during the current period

Therefore for a stationary demand distribution, $\hat{y}_{t+T}$, the forecast made in period t of the average demand for any future period T periods ahead is equal to the exponentially weighted average, i.e.

$$\hat{y}_{t+T} = u_t \tag{2.3}$$

Having defined the exponentially weighted average it is now possible to examine its advantages over the moving average. These advantages are as follows:

(a) Only one piece of information need be retained between forecasts; that is u_t which becomes u_{t-1} when the next forecast is made. For the moving average $n-1$ pieces of information must be retained, n being the number of time periods on which the moving average is based.

(b) The sensitivity of the exponentially weighted average can be altered at any time by changing the value of α. An increased value of α gives more weight to recent data and, therefore, makes the average more sensitive. Conversely a smaller value of α gives less weight to recent data and makes the average less sensitive to the data. For the moving average, the sensitivity can only be altered by changing n, the number of time periods on which the moving average is based, and this cannot generally be effected over a single time period as with the exponentially weighted average.

Brown[1] has indicated that the value of α used in forming an exponentially weighted average should not usually exceed 0·3, and that if it appears that a higher value of α is required, the assumption that y_t is drawn from a stationary distribution is likely to be invalid. However, although this ruling is an interesting generalisation, in practice one should always examine the forecasts produced by several values of α and choose that which produces the best forecast for the purpose for which it is being used. In many instances though, values of either 0·2 or 0·1 appear to be most popular.

When comparing the properties of moving averages with exponentially weighted averages, Brown has also shown that if two averages have the same sensitivity or 'average age of data' (where the average age is defined as the age of each piece of data used in forming the average, weighted as the data of that age would be weighted), then

$$\frac{1-\alpha}{\alpha} = \frac{n-1}{2}$$

Hence, an exponentially weighted average using the value of $\alpha = 0\cdot1$ (a value, as stated previously, much used in practice) can be regarded by the above criteria as being similar to a moving average drawing its data from 19 time periods. This emphasises the major drawback of the moving average as an estimator of the average demand per unit time; namely the vast amount of data that must be stored for fresh estimates to be made.

Kay and Hampton[2] in their comparison of moving and exponentially weighted averages applied to various series of demand data, concluded that although exponentially weighted averages generally appeared to produce smaller forecasting errors, the results obtained showed that the differences between these errors and those produced by the method of moving averages were rarely statistically significant. However, the relative costs involved when using exponentially weighted averages demonstrated in practical situations that this technique was somewhat superior to the method of moving averages for forecasting purpose. A small saving grace of the moving average is that when a regular seasonal effect influences the demand data, a moving average based on the same number of time periods as are included within the season will tend to reduce forecasting errors as compared with an exponentially weighted average. For example a twelve month moving average based on monthly data will tend to produce less forecasting errors when data is subject to an annual seasonal effect than an equivalent exponentially weighted average with $\alpha = 0\cdot154$.

Again, as with the method of moving averages, when beginning

Table 2.2. FORECASTING USING EXPONENTIALLY WEIGHTED AVERAGES

	Jan	Feb	Mar	Apr	May	Jun	Jul	Aug	Sep	Oct	Nov	Dec	Sum of squared forecasting errors
Monthly demand	48	60	50	72	80	60	66	72	80	61	65	75	
Exponentially weighted average with α = 0·1 and no initial estimate*	0	5	10	14	20	26	30	33	37	41	44	46	21 198
Exponentially weighted average with α = 0·1 and an initial estimate of 50*	50	50	51	51	53	56	57	59	59	61	61	62	2 223

* Note that the values calculated are shown in the month for which the forecast was intended although in fact this value was calculated in the previous month. For example, for the exponentially weighted average with an initial estimate of 50 the value calculated in February as (0·1×60+0·9×50) = 51, is entered for the month of March as this was the month for which a forecast of 51 was attempting to predict what the demand would be. The demand for this month was in fact 50, thus producing a forecasting error of 1.

a forecasting system with the exponentially weighted average method, an initial estimate will reduce the forecasting errors over the initialisation period. Table 2.2 illustrates such forecasts (based on the same data as used previously for the moving average method in Table 2.1) but this time using an exponentially weighted average with a value of $\alpha = 0.1$.

Comparing the forecasting errors produced, both by the method of exponentially weighted averages and moving averages (using the same criteria of the sum of squared errors), it can be seen that with no initial estimate the exponentially weighted average method produces a very high sum of squared forecasting errors (21 198) comparable with that due to the true six month moving average also with no initial estimate (24 007). With an initial estimate of 50 though, the exponentially weighted average produces a sum of squared forecasting errors (2 223) which in this particular case is bettered only by the initialised moving average with also an initial estimate of 50 (1 058).

In conclusion it would appear that the method of using exponentially weighted averages for forecasting is superior to that of moving averages, for the following reasons:

(a) Less data are required to be stored
(b) Only one initial estimate is required as opposed to $n-1$
(c) The rate of response of the average can be easily adjusted by varying the value of α
(d) Past data are rejected gradually rather than suddenly
(e) It is slightly easier to calculate see Fig. 2.1.

EXPONENTIALLY WEIGHTED AVERAGE ALLOWING FOR GROWTH

As has been explained earlier, both the method of moving averages and that of exponentially weighted averages assume that the mean value of the demand data does not vary with time, i.e. that the demand distribution is stationary. Where this assumption is known not to be true, some attempt must be made to estimate the rate of growth (or

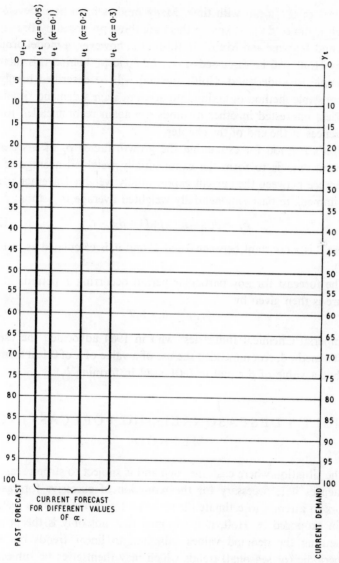

Fig. 2.1. Nomogram for calculating forecasts based on simple exponentially weighted averages

Instructions: Draw straight line between relevant values of u_{t-1} and y_t and read off new value of u_t on appropriate scale.

decline) of the mean with time. Many models have been developed which claim to do this, among them are those proposed by Brown,[1, 3] Box and Jenkins[4] and Muir.[5] In this book, however, a model proposed by Holt[6] will be discussed since the concept behind this method is simple to understand. Holt's method will be described briefly as one possible method of taking into account such a demand situation. Readers interested in other methods are again recommended to the references at the end of the chapter.

Holt's method for estimating the growth factor b_t of a series of demand data is to form the exponentially weighted average of the difference between the current exponentially weighted average u_t and the immediate past exponentially weighted average u_{t-1} thus:

$$b_t = \beta(u_t - u_{t-1}) + (1-\beta)b_{t-1} \tag{2.4}$$

where β is a constant between 0 and 1, and u_t is calculated as in Eqn. (1.2).

The forecast for any particular period occurring T periods in the future is then given by

$$\hat{y}_{t+T} = u_t + b_t T \tag{2.5}$$

Imperial Chemical Industries[7] who in 1964 advocated the use of Holt's method, recommended the use of a value of α of 0·1 in forming u_t, but a value of β equal to 0·01 used in forming b_t.

HOLT'S DESEASONALISING FORECASTING METHOD

In the situation where customer demand is subject to strong seasonal influences it is necessary for the reduction of excessive forecasting errors to attempt to estimate the seasonal trend factors. In a method again proposed by Holt, it is assumed that not only is the process generating the demand values subjected to linear trends but also to periodic (or seasonal) trends which may themselves be subject to trends.

Holt maintains that not to take into account a linear trend in demand patterns subjected to seasonal fluctuations necessarily means that any linear trend effect will automatically be incorporated in the deseasonalising factors which will then become unduly biased. Holt therefore, incorporates a linear trend factor in his exponentially smoothed average before estimating the deseasonalising factors thus:

$$u_t = \frac{\alpha y_t}{F_{t-K}} + (1-\alpha)(u_{t-1} + b_{t-1}) \tag{2.6}$$

where F_{t-K} is the smoothed deseasonalising factor calculated at the corresponding period of the last seasonal cycle (K being the number of time periods in the seasonal cycle), and

$$F_t = \frac{\gamma y_t}{u_t} + (1-\gamma)F_{t-K} \tag{2.7}$$

the linear trend factor is then calculated as usual by

$$b_t = \beta(u_t - u_{t-1}) + (1-\beta)b_{t-1} \tag{2.8}$$

and the forecast for period $t+T$ is given by

$$\hat{y}_{t+T} = (u_t + b_t T)F_{t-K+T} \tag{2.9}$$

where F_{t-K+T} is the last calculated deseasonalising factor corresponding to the period $t+T$. Winter[8] found that for several demand distributions values of α, γ and β equal to 0·2, 0·6 and 0·2 respectively produced a minimum standard deviation of forecasting errors.

Deseasonalising methods have several disadvantages, which are
  (a) Smoothed estimates of deseasonalising factors are calculated (for a particular period) very infrequently.
  (b) Errors are magnified in forecasts by the deseasonalising factors, hence this system breaks down if there are anything but small fluctuations in demand about the seasonal trend.
  (c) As many deseasonalising factors as there are periods in the season have to be stored.

ESTIMATING THE STANDARD DEVIATION OF DEMAND PER UNIT TIME

The statistical definition of the standard deviation is that it is the square root of the sum of the squared differences of a function from its mean divided by the number of degrees of freedom. This rather complicated definition, when applied to the forecasting situations being considered here, would entail summing together the squared values of the forecasting errors (perhaps on a moving average basis) and then dividing this sum by the degrees of freedom available, and then taking the square root. The degrees of freedom here would be the number of pieces of information that make up the sum less one. Such a computation at each and every forecast period is obviously out of the question and, if possible, a much simpler method of calculating the standard deviation (σ_t) should be used.

Fortunately, if great accuracy is not demanded, a possible method of calculating an estimate of the standard deviation of forecasting errors is to use a relationship that holds true for a large number of mathematical probability distributions; namely that the standard deviation is approximately equal to 1·25 times the mean absolute deviation.

The mean absolute deviation (m_t) is defined as the average of the absolute forecasting errors, *absolute* indicating that one regards the error always as positive irrespective of its actual polarity. It has already been shown that an exponentially weighted average is a true average so there is now no reason why the exponentially weighted average of the absolute forecasting errors should not be formed to produce the mean absolute deviation. Having formed this estimate of the mean absolute deviation, it is a simple matter to multiply this value by 1·25 to form an estimate of the standard deviation.

Describing this operation in equation form, the forecasting error at time t is given by

$$e_t = y_t - \hat{y}_t \tag{2.10}$$

and the mean absolute deviation is given by

$$m_t = \alpha \, |e_t| + (1-\alpha)m_{t-1} \tag{2.11}$$

Thus the standard deviation is estimated as

$$\sigma_t = 1 \cdot 25 m_t \tag{2.12}$$

Having estimated the value of the standard deviation of forecasting errors, this same value can be used as an estimate of the standard deviation of demand per unit time.

Table 2.3. A TYPICAL FORECASTING SCHEDULE ($\alpha = 0.2$)

		Jan	Feb	Mar	Apr	May	Jun	Jul	Aug	Sep	Oct	Nov	Dec	Jan
A	This month's demand		60	70	55	80	90	65	70	75	60	80	90	100	95
B	Last month's forecast for this month		70*	68	68	65	68	72	71	71	72	70	72	76	81
C	This month's forecasting error	A − B	−10	2	−13	15	22	−7	−1	4	−12	10	18	24	14
D	$\alpha\times$ this month's demand	$\alpha \times$ A	12	14	11	16	18	13	14	15	12	16	18	20	19
E	$(1-\alpha)\times$ last month's forecast for this month	$(1-\alpha)\times$ B	56	54	54	52	54	58	57	57	58	56	58	61	65
F	This month's forecast for next month	D + E	68	68	65	68	72	71	71	72	70	72	76	81	84

Table 2.3 *cont.*

		Jan	Feb	Mar	Apr	May	Jun	Jul	Aug	Sep	Oct	Nov	Dec	Jan
G	$\alpha \times$ modulus of this month's forecasting error	$\alpha \times |C|$	2·00	0·40	2·60	3·00	3·60	1·40	0	0·80	2·40	2·00	3·60	4·00	2·80
H	$(1-\alpha) \times$ last month's M.A.D	$(1-\alpha) \times I$ last	0*	1·60	1·60	3·37	5·10	7·00	6·70	5·35	4·92	5·85	6·30	7·90	9·50
I	This month's M.A.D	$G+H$	2·00	2·00	4·20	6·37	8·70	8·40	6·70	6·15	7·32	7·85	9·90	11·9	12·3
J	Standard deviation estimate	1·25 I	2·5	2·5	5·2	8·0	10·8	10·5	8·4	7·7	9·1	9·8	12·4	15·0	15·4

* Estimate

Table 2.3 shows a typical forecasting schedule where both the forecasts estimating the average demand and the standard deviation of demand are calculated. For the reader's convenience each row is labelled and the methods by which the values in each of those rows are evaluated are shown. Note that if an initial estimate for the mean absolute deviation other than zero were used, the estimated values for the standard deviation would stabilise more rapidly.

MONITORING A FORECASTING SYSTEM

When any routine forecasting system is set up within a business, it is highly desirable to incorporate some form of automatic monitoring method to ensure that the system remains in control. When unsuspected seasonal variations or a step change in demand (indicating a change in the average level of demand per unit time) occur, such alterations in the demand data introduce biased errors into the forecasts being made. It is apparent that such situations should be sensed as quickly as possible so that appropriate remedial action may be taken.

There have been several methods proposed for monitoring the stability of forecasts, but the two that have gained general acceptance are those due to Harrison and Davies[9] and to Trigg.[10] The method proposed by Harrison and Davies is an adaption of the traditional Cusum method. Although very sensitive and capable of providing more information of the changes that have occurred in the demand data, it is slightly more complicated than Trigg's method and will, therefore, not be discussed further here.

Trigg's method of monitoring (sometimes referred to as the smoothed error method) depends on the generation of a 'tracking signal' whose value, by definition, cannot exceed ± 1. When the tracking signal exceeds certain absolute levels, one can assess with a certain known degree of statistical confidence (a 95 per cent degree of confidence indicates that, on average, an event of this type will occur 19 times out of 20) that a change in the demand data has occurred. The tracking signal does not indicate the type of change, its purpose being to simply draw attention to the item concerned for closer scrutiny.

The tracking signal used in Trigg's method of monitoring is defined as the exponentially weighted average of the forecasting errors divided by the mean absolute deviation.

The mean absolute deviation (m_t) has already been defined by Eqn. (2.11) and the exponentially weighted average of forecasting errors ($\bar{e}_t$) is given by

$$\bar{e}_t = \alpha e_t + (1-\alpha)\bar{e}_{t-1} \tag{2.13}$$

and the tracking signal is then simply evaluated as T_t thus:

$$T_t = \bar{e}_t/m_t \tag{2.14}$$

It should be noted that although the formulae for evaluating the mean absolute deviation and the exponentially weighted average of forecasting errors look the same, in the former the absolute value of the error, $|e_t|$, is used but in the latter the true value of the error, e_t. The value of α in both these formulae should be the same and is usually chosen as either 0·1 or 0·2. Confidence limits of the value of the tracking signal, which if exceeded indicate a basic change in the demand data with a degree of confidence indicated, are given in Table 2.4.

Table 2.4. CONFIDENCE LIMITS OF TRIGG'S TRACKING SIGNAL

Cumulative probability (%)	Trigg's tracking signal (T_t)	
	$\alpha = 0·1$	$\alpha = 0·2$
0	0·0	0·0
50	0·21	0·32
70	0·30	0·46
80	0·36	0·54
90	0·45	0·66
95	0·51	0·74
100	1·00	1·00

The above confidence limits assume that the forecasting errors are normally distributed about the mean (see later concerning Normality). Defining the forecasting error as in Eqn. (2.6), i.e. as the actual demand

Table 2.5. A TYPICAL FORECASTING SCHEDULE ($\alpha = 0.2$)

		Jan	Feb	Mar	Apr	May	Jun	Jul	Aug	Sep	Oct	Nov	Dec	Jan
A	This month's demand	60	70	55	80	90	65	70	75	60	80	90	100	95
B	Last month's forecast for this month	70*	68	68	65	68	72	71	71	72	70	72	76	81
C	This month's forecasting error	A−B	−10	2	−13	15	22	−7	−1	4	−12	10	18	24	14
D	$\alpha \times$ this month's demand	$\alpha \times$ A	12	14	11	16	18	13	14	15	12	16	18	20	19
E	$(1-\alpha) \times$ last month's forecast for this month	$(1-\alpha) \times$ B	56	54	54	52	54	58	57	57	58	56	58	61	65
F	this month's forecast for next month	D+E	68	68	65	68	72	71	71	72	70	72	76	81	84
G	$\alpha \times$ this month's forecasting error	$\alpha \times$ C	−2·0	0·4	−2·6	3·0	3·6	−1·4	0	0·8	−2·4	2·0	3·6	4·0	2·8

Table 2.5. cont.

			Jan	Feb	Mar	Apr	May	Jun	Jul	Aug	Sep	Oct	Nov	Dec	Jan
H	$(1-\alpha)\times$last month's smoothed error	$(1-\alpha)\times$I last	0*	−1·60	−0·96	−2·85	0·01	2·90	1·20	0·96	1·40	0·80	0·94	3·55	6·02
I	This month's smoothed error	G+H	−2·00	−1·20	−3·56	0·15	3·61	1·50	1·20	1·76	−1·00	1·20	4·45	7·58	8·82
J	$\alpha\times$modulus of this month's forecasting error	$\alpha\times$|C|	2·00	0·40	2·60	3·00	3·60	1·40	0·0	0·80	2·40	2·00	3·60	4·00	2·80
K	$(1-\alpha)\times$last month's M.A.D.	$(1-\alpha)\times$L last	0*	1·60	1·60	3·37	5·10	7·00	6·70	5·35	4·92	5·85	6·30	7·90	9·50
L	This month's M.A.D.	J+K	2·00	2·00	4·20	6·37	8·70	8·40	6·70	6·15	7·32	7·85	9·90	11·9	12·3
M	Trigg's tracking signal	I/L	−1·00	−0·60	−0·85	−0·03	−0·42	0·18	0·18	0·29	−0·13	0·15	0·44	0·63	0·72
N	Standard deviation estimate	1·25 L	2·5	2·5	5·2	8·0	10·8	10·5	8·4	7·7	9·1	9·8	12·4	15·0	15·4

*Estimate

less the forecast, a positive value of the tracking signal indicates a rise in demand and a negative value a slackening of demand.

An example of how the tracking signal is used in practice, would be that if with a value of $\alpha = 0\cdot2$ the calculated value of the tracking signal exceeded $0\cdot74$, one would be 95 per cent confident (sure in 19 cases out of 20) that a significant *rise* in the average demand level had occurred.

Table 2.5 shows a fully expanded forecasting schedule which in addition to the figures shown in Table 2.4 shows the calculation of the exponentially weighted average of the forecasting errors and the value of Trigg's tracking signal. It will be noted that the tracking signal remains high during the first three months for which forecasts are made while the forecasting system settles down, but subsequently

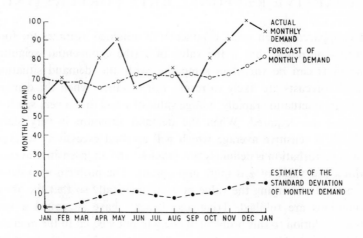

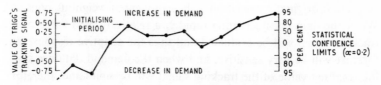

Fig. 2.2. A graphical plot of parameters from a typical forecasting schedule

remains at relatively low values until the month of December. Then in December, a value of $+0.63$ for Trigg's tracking signal indicates that the demand of 90 in the previous month of November and the current demand of 100 have raised the average level of demand above that existing up to that time (i.e. during the months January through to October). This value of 0.63 indicates that one can be nearly 90 per cent sure that this is the case, and the subsequent value of 0.72 occurring in January due to another high demand value reaffirms this assumption as being now nearly 95 per cent certain. Fig. 2.2 illustrates the data of Table 2.5 in graphical form to show more clearly the relationship of the various parameters obtained from the fully expanded forecasting schedule.

ADAPTIVE RESPONSE RATE FORECASTING

It is apparent when using exponentially weighted averages for forecasting purposes, that if the value of α (the exponential weighting constant) can be varied in sympathy with the demand situation, better forecasts are likely to result. For instance, when the demand data are fluctuating rapidly, a large value of α and thus a very sensitive average are required. When the demand situation is very stable though, a sensitive average which will respond excessively to every small perturbation is definitely not required and an insensitive average with a low value of α is more appropriate. The problem is to devise a method of varying the value of α automatically so that the above conditions are fulfilled. Trigg and Leach[11] have suggested a very simple solution to this problem, namely to put α equal to the modulus of Trigg's tracking signal. This is obviously feasible as the modulus of Trigg's tracking signal can only vary between 0 and 1 which is the restriction originally placed on α the exponential weighting constant. When the data are fluctuating rapidly, a relatively high value of the tracking signal will be evaluated and thus the adaptive response rate forecast will be very sensitive, and when the demand data are stable the resulting value of the tracking signal will be small and, therefore, a very stable forecast will be generated.

This adaptive response rate forecast is defined by

$$\hat{y}_{t+T} = \tilde{u}_t = |T_t| y_t + (1 - |T_t|)\tilde{u}_{t-1} \qquad (2.15)$$

and it has been further pointed out that if the last calculated value of the tracking signal is used rather than the current value, then spurious responses to single period demand impulses can be avoided without impairing the general overall response of the adaptive forecast, thus

$$\hat{y}_{t+T} = \tilde{u}_t = |T_{t-1}| y_t + (1 - |T_{t-1}|)\tilde{u}_{t-1} \qquad (2.16)$$

The improved response to a sudden step change in demand of an adaptive response rate forecast as defined by Eqn. (2.15) (using $\alpha = 0\cdot1$

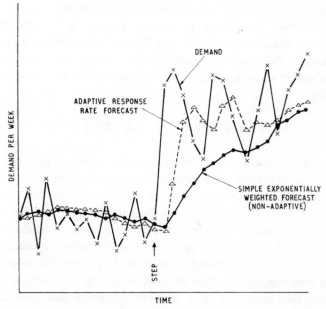

Fig. 2.3. Comparison of simple and adaptive response rate forecasts to a step function

only in forming the tracking signal) over a forecast based on a simple exponentially weighted average with $\alpha = 0\cdot1$, is shown in Fig. 2.3.

Trigg and Leach indicate that because forecasting errors are radically reduced when using adaptive forecasting, the statistical significance of the value of the tracking signal is no longer maintained. Although there are many arguments for relying on manual intervention of forecasting systems when this is indicated as necessary by a tracking signal *with* confidence limits, it would appear that where forecasts are made by computer for a large number of items, many of which may be small runners (of low unit cost), it would seem on balance to be better for the system to take automatic remedial action by adaptive response rate forecasts. If it is required to gain the advantages of both the adaptive forecast's reduced forecasting errors and the non-adaptive forecast's statistical monitoring possibilities, one can calculate the adaptive forecast actually to predict and generate a non-adaptive forecast solely to form the tracking signal.

The method of adaptive response rate forecasting is particularly valuable when initiating a forecasting system. It is sufficient to make only crude guesses at the coefficients in the forecasting model and even if these are wildly wrong, the tracking signal will tend to high absolute values and the system will 'home in' with corresponding rapidity.

STATISTICAL DISTRIBUTIONS

A 'frequency distribution' is an ordered arrangement of data from the smallest to the highest value included within the data. For convenience the values appearing in the data are grouped into classes of equal width (i.e. 1–10, 11–20, . . ., 41–50, etc.) and the height of each class indicates the number of values that have occurred in the data lying in that particular class interval. A relative frequency distribution is one in which the height of each class interval represents the proportion of the total number of values included within the data sample which fall into that particular class. For any particular data sample, the frequency distribution will have the same shape as the relative frequency distribution and the latter can be obtained from the former simply by altering the scale of the vertical axis.

As an example consider the following data sample which represents the monthly demand for an item of stock over the past three years (i.e. 36 months).

Demand per month	Frequency of occurrence	Percentage probability of occurrence, (%)
1–10	4	11
11–20	7	19
21–30	6	17
31–40	12	33
41–50	5	14
greater than 50	2	6
	36	100

Fig. 2.4 shows this information plotted simultaneously as a frequency distribution (left-hand scale) and as a relative frequency distribution (right-hand scale).

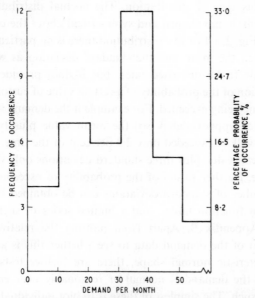

Fig. 2.4. Monthly demand data plotted as both a frequency distribution and relative frequency distribution

As has already been shown, the standard deviation is a measure of the variation of a series of data about its mean. It so happens that for certain relative frequency distributions which can be conveniently described by mathematical formulae, the probability of a particular value of the data occurring is related exactly to the standard deviation. Three such distributions will be discussed here since they often approximate to the type of distributions encountered in customer demand situations.

THE NORMAL DISTRIBUTION (APPENDIX B)

The normal distribution is one which will often provide an approximate fit to the demand distribution at factory level. This is because the averaging process which naturally takes place as customer orders are aggregated up from-retailer-to-wholesaler-to-factory, tends to produce this type of distribution. The normal distribution is characteristically hump shaped and symmetrical about the centre as can be seen in Fig. 2.5. For this distribution there is no particular relationship between the mean and the standard deviation as with the two distributions to be discussed later, but it does provide an explicit determination of the probability of a certain value of customer demand per unit time being exceeded. For example if the demand is distributed normally (or approximately so) the mean value plus two standard deviations will be exceeded only 2·3 per cent of the time, on average, and the mean value plus three standard deviations only 0·13 per cent of the time. Further values of the probability of exceeding the mean plus a number of standard deviations can be obtained from normal distribution function tables, and a limited series of such values are given in Appendix B. Apart from plotting the relative frequency distribution of the demand data to see whether this is anything like the characteristic normal shape, there are further tests which will indicate if the demand is normal or reasonably near enough to be treated as such. The simplest of these is to plot individual class values of the cumulative probability of occurrence on normal probability paper and if the points lie approximately on a straight line then normality can be assumed. For those readers interested in statistical tests for goodness of fit, either the Kolmogorov-Smirnov or χ^2 test is suitable.

The true normal distribution is a continuous curve rather than a relative frequency distribution with discrete class intervals and, hence,

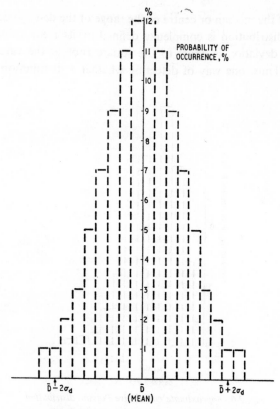

Fig. 2.5. *Approximate normal distribution*

theoretically the 'tails' of the normal distribution extend to minus infinity on the left-hand side and to plus infinity on the right. This fact should be kept in mind whenever the assumption of normality is made.

THE POISSON DISTRIBUTION (APPENDIX C)

A mathematical distribution which often approximates to the distribution of demand at the retailer level, is the Poisson distribution. The characteristic shape of the Poisson distribution (which is shown in Fig. 2.6) is 'skewed' to the left (i.e. the bulk of the distribution is to the left of the median or centre of the range of the demand data). The Poisson distribution is completely defined by its mean value, as the standard deviation is equal to the square root of the value of the average. Thus, one way of detecting whether a distribution is likely

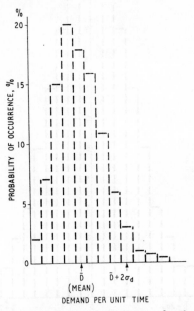

Fig. 2.6. Approximate cumulative Poisson distribution

to be approximately Poisson is to check that it is skewed to the left, and that the estimate of the standard deviation is approximately equal to the square root of the estimate of the mean. A reasonably good working rule for the Poisson distribution is that a demand value above the value of the mean plus two standard deviations will be exceeded (on average) 2 per cent of the time. Below a value of two standard deviations, however, the probabilities of exceeding specified values of demand depend very much on the particular distribution's average value. Generally, tables providing values of the summed Poisson distribution function do not include values for a mean value above 20. This is because the Poisson distribution is usually applied only to distributions covering a fairly narrow range of low average values.

THE EXPONENTIAL DISTRIBUTION
(APPENDIX D)

Another mathematical distribution which may often provide an approximate fit to demand data at the retailer or wholesaler level is the exponential distribution. The exponential distribution (whose characteristic shape is shown in Fig. 2.7) like the Poisson distribution

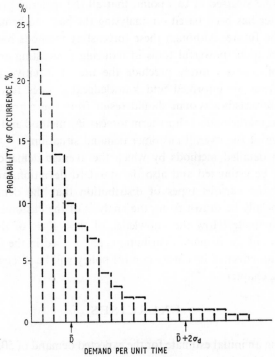

Fig. 2.7. Approximate exponential distribution

has a simple convenient relationship between its average and standard deviation, namely that they are equal. Two reasonably good working rules for this distribution are: a demand value will (on average) exceed a value of the mean plus two standard deviations (i.e. a value three times the mean) 5 per cent of the time; and a value of the mean

4

plus one standard deviation 13·5 per cent of the time. As with the Poisson distribution, a method of detecting whether a distribution is likely to be approximately exponential is to check that the characteristic shape is evident and that the standard deviation here is equal to the mean.

CONCLUSION

It should be stressed at this point, that all the material presented in this chapter has been based on analysing the past mathematically to predict the future. Although these forecasting methods have proved themselves to be powerful tools in reducing forecasting errors, they do not of course entirely preclude the use of intuitive judgement derived from an informed and knowledgeable sales force. Ideally the best forecasting system should result from the correct blending of a sound mathematical short-term forecasting method and a detailed knowledge of the overall customer demand situation.

Having detailed methods by which the average demand per unit time may be estimated and also the standard deviation, and having described the various types of distribution that the demand data might typically be drawn from, the analysis of the customer demand is now complete. How the knowledge of the values of the various parameters of the demand distribution can be used in the implementation of an effective inventory control policy will be discussed in the remaining chapters.

EXERCISES

1. Using an initial estimate for the expected demand of 50, calculate the initialising six month moving average and the exponentially weighted average ($\alpha = 0.1$) as forecasts of the expected demand in the next month for the demand data provided. Which of the two methods in this particular case produces the better forecast?

Jan	Feb	Mar	Apr	May	Jun	Jul	Aug	Sep	Oct	Nov	Dec
30	35	25	40	30	35	40	40	50	70	70	65

Answer. The initialising six month moving average.

2. Show that Holt's method of forecasting for one month ahead (using values of $\alpha = 0.3$ and $\beta = 0.3$) provides a better forecast than a simple exponentially weighted average (using a value of $\alpha = 0.3$) when applied to the data provided. This data is particularly chosen because it is derived from a steadily expanding market situation. What is the percentage improvement in the sum of squared forecasting errors using Holt's method as opposed to the simple exponentially weighted average method?

Jan	Feb	Mar	Apr	May	Jun	Jul	Aug	Sep	Oct	Nov	Dec
10	19	31	42	50	59	71	83	88	101	113	120

Answer. Using no initial estimates, Holt's method is better, and provides an approximate 40 per cent reduction in the sum of squared forecasting errors as compared with the simple exponentially weighted average method.

3. In what month (after the initialising period) does the value of Trigg's tracking signal (based on a value of $\alpha = 0.1$) indicate that a significant rise in the average demand level has occurred (with a 90 per cent degree of confidence) when forecasts are based on a simple exponentially weighted average with the same value of α? Assume that in the previous month a forecast of 50 produced an exponentially weighted average error of 6 and a mean absolute deviation of 10.

Jan	Feb	Mar	Apr	May	Jun	Jul	Aug	Sep	Oct	Nov	Dec
55	60	40	45	50	51	46	80	85	81	79	76

Answer. The month of August as the value of T_t then exceeds 0.45.

REFERENCES

1. BROWN, R. G., *Statistical Forecasting for Inventory Control*, McGraw-Hill; New York (1959).
2. KAY, E. and HAMPTON, J. S., *An Experiment on Short-term Forecasting*. Paper presented to the International Federation of O.R. Societies, Oslo (July 1963).
3. BROWN, R. G., *Smoothing, Forecasting and Predictions of Discrete Time Series*, Prentice-Hall, New Jersey (1962).
4. BOX, G. E. P. and JENKINS, C. M., 'Some Statistical Aspects of Adaptive Optimization and Control, *J. roy. Stat. Soc.*, **24B,** 297 (1962).
5. MUIR, A., 'Automatic Sales Forecasting', *Comput J.*, **1,** 113 (1958).
6. HOLT, C. C., 'Forecasting Seasonals by Exponentially Weighted Moving Averages', *Office of Naval Research Memo*, No. 52 (1957).
7. IMPERICAL CHEMICAL INDUSTRIES, 'Short-term Forecasting', *I.C.I. Monograph* No. 2, Oliver & Boyd, Edinburgh (1964).
8. WINTER, P. R., 'Forecasting Sales by Exponentially Weighted Moving Averages' *Mgmt Sci.*, **6,** 324 (1960).
9. HARRISON, P. J. and DAVIES, O. L., 'The Use of Cumulative Sum (Cusum) Techniques for the Control of Routine Forecasts of Product Demand', *Ops Res.*, **12,** 325 (1964).
10. TRIGG, D. W., 'Monitoring a Forecasting System', *Opl Res. Q.*, **15,** 271 (1964).
11. TRIGG, D. W. and LEACH, A. G., 'Exponential Smoothing with an Adaptive Response Rate', *Opl Res. Q.*, **18,** 53 (1967).

Mathematical Tables

EILON, S., *Industrial Engineering Tables*, van Nostrand, London (1962).
LINDLEY, D. V. and MILLER, J. C. P., *Cambridge Elementary Statistical Tables*, Cambridge University Press (1961).
MURDOCH, J. and BARNES, J. A., *Statistical Tables for Science and Engineering*, Macmillan (1968).

CHAPTER 3

Re-order Level Policy: Separate Calculation of Re-order Levels and Replenishment Order Quantities

As has already been stated, the re-order level policy is that inventory policy in which a fixed quantity replenishment order is placed when the inventory held falls to, or below the re-order level. Thus, when operating the re-order level policy, there are only two parameters whose values must be decided, namely:

(a) The re-order level

(b) The replenishment order quantity

Before discussing the various methods of calculating values for the re-order level and the replenishment order quantity, some of the terms that will be used must be defined. These are:

$\bar{D}$ The average demand per unit time (as estimated using one of the forecasting methods described in the previous chapter)

σ_d The standard deviation of demand per unit time (estimated as 1·25 times the mean absolute deviation of demand per unit time)

$\bar{L}$ The average leadtime duration

σ_l The standard deviation of leadtime durations

M The re-order level

q The replenishment order size
C_m The material and labour cost or works prime cost of one unit of inventory
C_h The annual cost of holding one unit of inventory
C_o The cost of placing a replenishment order or the set-up cost involved in initiating a production run
C_a The selling price of one unit of inventory
A The annual usage, demand or sales for an inventory item (estimated using the average demand per unit time and the number of time units occurring in one year)
k Standard normal deviate

CALCULATION OF THE RE-ORDER LEVEL

The classical approach to calculating a value for the re-order level is to assume that the management of the business operating the inventory system will be prepared to allow a stockout to occur only occassionally and moreover that they will also be prepared to specify what that probability of stockout should be, on average.*

Given this naïve situation with a specified probability of stockout, it is then a relatively simple matter to calculate the requisite value of the re-order level required.

Re-order Level Required when the Demand per Unit Time is Variable but the Leadtime Duration is Fixed

Given the situation where it is known that the demand per unit time is distributed approximately as to a mathematical probability distribution, with a mean and standard deviation of $\bar{D}$ and σ_d respectively, and that the leadtime is of fixed duration (i.e. $\bar{L}$ is constant and $\sigma_l = 0$), then the re-order level which will provide, on average, a fixed probability of stockout will be equal to the maximum reasonable expected demand during the leadtime.

* The probability of not running out is known as the 'service level'.

This maximum expected demand during the leadtime can be considered as being made up of two sections, these being the average demand during the leadtime plus an additional amount which only occurs when the demand during the leadtime is greater than average.

This additional amount of inventory required (when incorporated as part of the re-order level) to prevent excessive stockouts occurring for higher than average demand situations, is known as the safety (or sometimes buffer) stock.

Thus:

Re-order level = average demand during the leadtime + safety stock

In a situation where the demand per unit time is distributed approximately as a normal distribution this can be expressed mathematically as:

$$M = \bar{D}\bar{L} + k\sigma_d \sqrt{L} \qquad (3.1)$$

where k is known as the standard normal deviate, and it is this value of k which determines what the service level or probability of a stockout occurring will be. Values for k and the corresponding probability of stockout or service level can be found in normal probability tables (see Appendix B), but the following values will give some indication of what level of service is provided for $k = 1, 2$ and 3.

If $k = 1$, a stockout will occur on average 15·9 per cent of the time
$k = 2$, a stockout will occur on average 2·3 per cent of the time
$k = 3$, a stockout will occur on average 0·1 per cent of the time

For both the Poisson and exponential distributions the probabilities of a stockout occurring can be read directly from tables using $\bar{D}\bar{L}$ as the average value quoted for these tables.

Alternatively, these values can be calculated using the following formulae:

Probability of stockout when demand is Poisson $= \sum\limits_{M}^{\infty} \dfrac{(\bar{D}\bar{L})^M e^{-\bar{D}\bar{L}}}{M!}$

(see Appendix C)

Probability of stockout when demand is exponential $= e^{-M/\bar{D}\bar{L}}$

(see Appendix D)

The latter can be evaluated quite simply on a slide-rule provided with log-log scales. As an example, Table 3.1 indicates the probabilities of stockouts occurring when the demand during the leadtime is distributed approximately either as a Poisson or as an exponential distribution, both with an average value of three units.

Table 3.1. PROBABILITY OF STOCKOUT FOR A POISSON AND EXPONENTIAL DISTRIBUTION WITH AN AVERAGE VALUE OF 3

Re-order level (ROL)	Probability of a stockout occurring, $\bar{D}L = 3$	
	Poisson	*Exponential*
3	35·3	36·8
4	18·5	26·3
5	8·4	19·2
6	3·3	13·5
7	1·2	10·0
8	0·4	7·4

It should be noted at this point, that the sole purpose of the safety stock is to prevent stockouts from occurring. Because the average demand during the leadtime is, however, exceeded for only some specified proportion of the time this means that the safety stock will also be used only for this same proportion of the time. Thus, in deciding a suitable level of service, management should weigh the cost of holding this amount of under-utilised safety stock against the cost of stockout and also the cost of ordering replenishments. Unfortunately, this 'level of service' approach does not allow for this, other than through intuitive judgement, but even so the method is much used in practice.

Re-order Level Required When Demand and Leadtime Durations are Both Variable

When leadtime durations and the demand per unit time vary considerably, calculation of the re-order levels required to give certain levels of service becomes more complicated. The reason for this is that the demand during the leadtime can now be higher than average for more than one reason, the most likely being:

(*a*) Higher than average demand occurring during an average leadtime period (as in the previous case discussed)

(*b*) Average demand occurring during a longer than average lead-time period

(*c*) Higher than average demand occurring during a longer than average leadtime period

Three possible approaches to this problem of evaluating the values of re-order levels required to maintain certain levels of service with variable leadtimes are:

(*a*) If both the demand per unit time and the leadtime durations are distributed to a known mathematical probability distribution (or approximately so), values of the probability of exceeding certain levels can be found in 'bivariate' probability distribution tables. Care, however, must be taken to prevent results from being unduly biased when using these. Tables exist for the situation where two indepen-dent variables or two variables with a known degree of correla-tion are both distributed normally. Unfortunately, in the customer demand situation the assumptions required to use such tables are not often met, and so this method is not often used.

(*b*) If the demand per unit time is distributed (approximately) as a known mathematical probability distribution and the different values of the leadtime durations are few in number and occur with a known probability, an iterative computation procedure can be used to evalu-ate the value of the re-order level. As an example of this method, consider the following problem:

Given that the demand per week is distributed normally with an average value of 50 and a standard deviation of 37·5, also that the probability of specific leadtimes occurring is as shown in Table 3.2, what service level will be afforded by a re-order level of 300 units?

By transposing Eqn. (3.1), one can calculate the value of the normal deviate k for each and every leadtime given in Table 3.2, thus

$$k = \frac{M - \bar{D}L}{\sigma_d \sqrt{L}} \tag{3.2}$$

where $M = 300$ units, $\bar{D} = 50$ units/week,

$\sigma_d =$ units/week and $L = 1, 2, 3, 4$ and 5 weeks

Table 3.2. PROBABILITIES OF OCCURRENCE
FOR LEADTIMES

Leadtime duration, weeks	Probability of occurrence, %
1	10
2	20
3	40
4	20
5	10

Having calculated k for every possible leadtime, one can then find from normal probability tables the appropriate service levels afforded by a re-order level of 300 for each of these leadtimes, should they occur. Knowing the service levels appropriate to each leadtime, one can then calculate the conditional probability of not running out of stock for each by multiplying the service level by the probability of that leadtime occurring. By summing together all these conditional probabilities of not running out, the overall service level is evaluated. Table 3.3 shows these calculations performed in a step-by-step procedure. The result shows for the situation where a normally distributed demand of average 50 units and standard deviation of 37·5 units occurs during leadtimes whose probability of occurrence is as in Table 3.2, that a re-order level of 300 will on average give a 95·36 per cent service level.

(*c*) If both the demand and leadtimes can be assumed to be distributed approximately normally and also independently of each other, then Eqn. (3.1) can be modified to take into account the variability of the leadtimes, thus

$$M = \bar{D}\bar{L} + k\sqrt{(\bar{L}\sigma_d^2 + \bar{D}^2\sigma_l^2)} \tag{3.3}$$

Like approach (*a*), this model is theoretically somewhat restricted in application because, as has been mentioned, the assumption of

Table 3.3. Iterative method of calculating service level for the re-order level policy when the demand per unit time is distributed normally and the distribution of leadtimes is known

Leadtime	Value of k when $M = 300$	A — Probability of not running out of stock corresponding to the value of k calculated, %	B — Probability of this particular leadtime occurring, %	A×B — Conditional probability of not running out of stock, %
1	$\dfrac{300-50}{37 \cdot 5 \sqrt{1}} = 6 \cdot 67$	100·0	10·0	10·0
2	$\dfrac{300-100}{37 \cdot 5 \sqrt{2}} = 3 \cdot 78$	100·0	20·0	20·0
3	$\dfrac{300-150}{37 \cdot 5 \sqrt{3}} = 2 \cdot 31$	98·9	40·0	39·96
4	$\dfrac{300-200}{37 \cdot 5 \sqrt{4}} = 1 \cdot 34$	91·0	20·0	18·20
5	$\dfrac{300-250}{37 \cdot 5 \sqrt{5}} = 0 \cdot 59$	72·0	10·0	7·20
			Total and overall service level	95·36

normality for the leadtime duration is often not valid, the bivariate distribution is not itself normally distributed, and also because the demand per unit time and the length of leadtimes are often not independent of each other. A situation of general high demand in a trade is often typified by longer than usual leadtimes due to the general increase in market activity and conversely low demand situations may often produce shorter than usual leadtimes. When such conditions do occur there is obviously a strong *correlation* (i.e. statistical dependence) between demand per unit time and leadtime durations and this would to a certain extent invalidate the assumptions on which Eqn. (3.3) is based.

However, assuming that for the situation considered earlier, these assumptions are valid or at least reasonably so, applying Eqn. (3.3)—having calculated from the leadtime data that $\bar{L} = 3$ and $\sigma_l = 1 \cdot 45$—the value of the normal deviate k is evaluated as $2 \cdot 04$ thus:

$$k = \frac{M - \bar{D}\bar{L}}{\sqrt{(\bar{L}\sigma_d^2 + \bar{D}^2\sigma_l^2)}} \tag{3.4}$$

Therefore

$$k = \frac{300 - 50 \cdot 3}{\sqrt{[3(37 \cdot 5)^2 + (50)^2 (1 \cdot 45)^2]}}$$

$$k = \frac{150}{73 \cdot 7} = 2 \cdot 04$$

A value of k of $2 \cdot 04$ ensures (if demand during the leadtime is approximately normal) a service level of $97 \cdot 9$ per cent as compared with the $95 \cdot 36$ per cent level as calculated using the iterative method. The difference of the level of service afforded using this method of calculation is mainly due to the assumption of normality for the leadtime distribution.

Eqn. (3.3) can be very much simplified (see Lewis[1]) by making several reasonable assumptions, back into its original form but with a modified form of normal deviate k_o, thus:

$$M = \bar{D}\bar{L} + k_o \sigma_d \sqrt{L} \tag{3.5}$$

where k_o is calculated from Table 3.4 and is dependent only on the average leadtime $\bar{L}$.

Table 3.4. VALUES OF MODIFIED NORMAL DEVIATE k_o TO ACCOUNT
FOR LEADTIME VARIABILITY

$\bar{L}$	1	2	3	4	5	6	7	8
k_t	1·1k	1·1k	1·2k	1·2k	1·3k	1·3k	1·4k	1·4k

Although this method may at first sight not appear a great simplification, it does produce a very simple decision rule. This states that
when it can no longer be assumed that the leadtime duration is fixed;
to maintain the service level at approximately the same value as that
existing when the leadtime was fixed, increase the value of the re-order
level by an amount equal to between 10 and 40 per cent of the *safety
stocks* held, the precise percentage being fixed by the average leadtime
value through Table 3.4.

Applying this rule to the situation previously considered with
$k_o = 1\cdot2k$ as $\bar{L} = 3$, then

$$k = \frac{M - \bar{D}\bar{L}}{1\cdot2\sigma_d\sqrt{\bar{L}}}$$

and

$$k = \frac{300 - 50\cdot3}{1\cdot2(37\cdot5)\sqrt{3}}$$

$$k = 1\cdot92$$

A value of k of $1\cdot92$ ensures a service level of $97\cdot26$ per cent which
compares very favourably with the $97\cdot9$ per cent value as calculated
by the more complicated formula of Eqn. 3.4.

A summary of the values achieved by the various methods of
calculation on the same data, for the service level afforded by a re-
order level of 300 units is shown in Table 3.5.

There are several disadvantages in the concept of 'service levels'
for calculating re-order levels and also inaccuracies are caused by
some of the assumptions that are made, some of these are described
as follows:

(*a*) The service level, although defining the probability of not running out of stock does not indicate how frequently stockouts are
likely to occur in any given time period. For instance, a firm which
places replenishment orders on average once a month will, with a

Table. 3.5 SERVICE LEVELS AFFORDED AS CALCULATED FOR A RE-ORDER
LEVEL OF 300 USING THREE DIFFERENT METHODS

Method used	*Service level,* %
Iterative method assuming normality of demand per week only	95·36
Assumption of normality and independence for both demand and leadtimes	97·90
Simplified method assuming normality and independence for both	97·26

95 per cent service level, run out of stock approximately once in two years, whereas a firm operating with the same service level but placing replenishment orders on average once a week will run out of stock roughly five times in the same period.

(*b*) The service level concept does not of itself take into account the balancing of costs of holding the additional stocks required to reduce the frequency of stockouts against those costs involved in allowing such stockouts to occur. This cost appraisal is inferred only in a management's intuitive decision as to what level of service should exist.

(*c*) The value of the re-order level should be related to the value of the replenishment order quantity for optimum cost operation and not viewed in isolation. This is partially inferred in (*a*) above.

(*d*) Unless demand orders per unit time are of unit size (i.e. for one item of stock only), replenishment orders will very rarely be placed when the stock on-hand is *exactly* equal to the re-order level as has been assumed throughout the calculations just described. More often than not the stock on-hand will be considerably below the re-order level when an order for replenishment is initiated, and the amount by which the re-order level is broken is known as the 'overshoot'.

Fig. 3.1. shows a typical inventory balance situation for a re-order level policy and indicates how zero, medium and large overshoots can occur in practice.

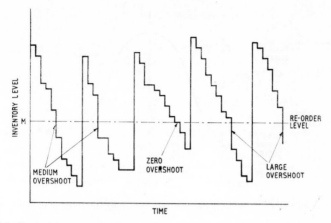

Fig. 3.1. Typical inventory balances for a re-order level policy indicating differing degrees of overshoot

Making certain assumptions it has been noted[2] that it is possible to evaluate the average overshoot $\bar{K}$ as

$$\bar{K} = \tfrac{1}{2}(\bar{D} - 1 + \sigma_d^2/\bar{D}) \qquad (3.6)$$

For the data considered previously the value of the average overshoot can be evaluated as 38·5 units of stock by

$$\bar{K} = \tfrac{1}{2}\{50 - 1 + (37\cdot5)^2/50\}$$
$$\bar{K} = 77/2 = 38\cdot5$$

Thus, in practice, the re-order level should be set at 338·5 units rather than 300 to achieve the desired service level.

Note. Strictly speaking, the $\bar{D}$ and σ_d of Eqn. (3.6) refer to an analysis of individual customer demand orders and not demand per unit time. However, in a practical situation if this unit of time is considerably less than the leadtime duration as is usually the case, the two can be considered as the same.

(*e*) The assumption that demand per unit time is distributed normally means, in theory, that demand values can extend to both plus and minus infinity although the probabilities of occurrence at these extremes are very small. But in this situation it is apparent that demand can become negative, indicating that stock is returned to stores rather

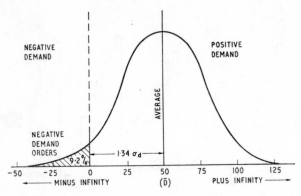

Fig. 3.2. Normal distribution of demand indicating the occurrence of negative demand

than removed. Although this return of stock can happen in practice this is not usually so. Therefore, by assuming that the demand is distributed normally, automatically by definition, negative demand is assumed to exist and this factor has the effect of reducing the average demand slightly below its stated value. The effect of this is to again make the re-order level lower than it should be if all demand were considered positive. This effect in conjunction with that caused by overshoot will ensure that calculated re-order levels are lower than they should be in practice to achieve a stated level of service.

Although it is not possible to relate directly the degree of inaccuracy caused to the calculated value of the re-order level as a result of the assumption of normality, it is possible to estimate the proportion of demand orders that are negative whenever this assumption is made. Fig. 3.2 shows the normal distribution considered earlier (i.e. with a mean of 50 and a standard deviation of 37·5). It is apparent that zero occurs at $50/37·5 = 1·34$ standard deviations below (i.e. to the left) of the average value 50. Looking up this value as k in normal probability tables indicates that the percentage of orders that occur below zero, and which are therefore by inference negative, is 9.2 per cent. Fortunately in this particular situation the proportion of negative orders is small enough not to cause too great an inaccuracy in the calculated re-order level, mainly because the sizes of the majority of these negative demand orders are small. Results obtained by simulation (see Chapter 10) indicate that the re-order level in this particular case should be raised by about an additional five units, that is from 338·5 units to 343·5 units, to offset this negative demand effect caused by the assumption of normality for the demand. In situations, however, where the average demand is low but the standard deviation relatively high it is apparent that a significantly higher proportion of demand orders will become negative if the assumption of normality is made, and it is in these situations that the resultant error caused by this effect cannot be ignored.

CALCULATION OF THE REPLENISHMENT ORDER QUANTITY

For the re-order level policy, the replenishment order quantity is a fixed size. In this section we shall consider what value this fixed replenishment order quantity should be.

Economic Order Quantity

As early as 1929, Wilson[3] proposed his 'economic order quantity' formulation for calculating the replenishment order size. In its simplest presentation this method is based on the assumption that the cost of managing inventory is made up of only two parts, namely the cost of placing replenishment orders and the cost of holding stock.

ORDERING COSTS

It is assumed that the cost of placing a replenishment order (C_o) is independent of the actual size (q) of the replenishment order (i.e. it costs as much to place an order for 100 as for a 1 000) and that, therefore, the cost of ordering per item of stock is C_o/q. Thus the annual ordering costs involved for an annual sales turnover of A is given by AC_o/q, the annual sales being evaluated usually from the average demand per unit time.

HOLDING COSTS

These include the costs of actually storing goods, such as storemen's wages, warehouse expenses, deterioration, etc. The opportunity costs of money tied up in inventory should also be included as part of the overall holding costs.

In the simple cost model considered here, it is assumed that the cost of holding stocks is directly proportional to the average amount of stock held.

For the purposes of evaluating this average amount of stock held, it is convenient to consider the stock to be made up of both *active* and *safety* stock. As the name implies, active stock is that which in the normal course of events is utilised continuously and can, therefore, be considered as any stock held other than the safety stock. Fig. 3.3 indicates a series of inventory balances for a re-order level policy where the demand during each leadtime is always average and thus the safety stock is never utilised. In this particular situation it is evident that if the replenishment order quantity is q, then the average value of the active stock is $q/2$. For the more realistic situation where

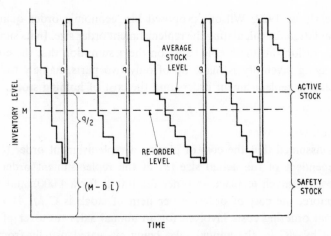

Fig. 3.3. Inventory balances for a re-order level policy in which demand during the leadtime is always average

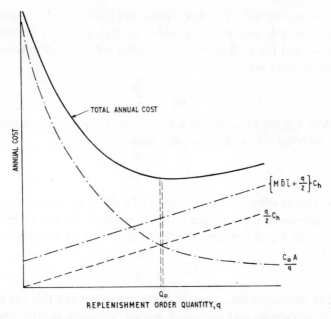

Fig. 3.4. Variation of total annual cost with replenishment order quantity

the active stock's maximum and minimum levels do not remain the same with each replenishment, $q/2$ still remains the best estimate of the average value of the active stock. As the safety stock is on average always held, the overall average value of the inventory level will be equal to $q/2$ plus the value of the safety stocks. If the re-order level M has been calculated to provide a known level of service, the average value of the safety stock is $(M - \bar{D}\bar{L})$. Thus the annual holding cost can be evaluated as

$$\text{annual holding costs} = (M - \bar{D}\bar{L} + q/2)C_h$$

and the total annual cost therefore as:

$$C = \frac{C_o A}{q} + (M - \bar{D}\bar{L} + q/2)C_h \qquad (3.7)$$

Fig. 3.4 shows graphically how each of these costs varies with q the replenishment order size, and it can be seen that the total annual

5*

cost is represented by a curve which has a minimum cost value. To find what this minimum cost value is, the expression for the total annual cost (Eqn. (3.7)) is differentiated with respect to q and put equal to zero, thus:

$$-\frac{C_o A}{q^2} + \frac{C_h}{2} = 0$$

And if q the variable replenishment order quantity is redefined as Q_o the 'economic order quantity', then

$$Q_o = \sqrt{\frac{2C_o A}{C_h}} \tag{3.8}$$

When, as often happens, the cost of holding an item of stock, C_h, is expressed as a percentage 'i' of the material and labour or works prime cost C_m of that item, then $C_h = iC_m$ and Eqn. (3.8) becomes

$$Q_o = \sqrt{\frac{2C_o A}{iC_m}} \tag{3.9}$$

The concept of the economic order quantity is one that has caused more discussion and argument among inventory control theorists than any other,[4, 5, 6] and an obvious criticism of the method is that the total annual cost formula does not take into account the cost of stockouts. However, as each criticism is levelled it is usually defended by a modification to the basic cost Eqn. (3.7) and, hence, a whole series of economic order equations has evolved. Although it is not possible here to discuss all these variants, some of the more important criticisms levelled at the method and how these have to some extent been accounted for will be discussed.

Minimum Economic Order Quantity

It is often argued that because the total annual cost curve is very flat, the increased total cost involved in placing replenishment orders for quantities either smaller or larger than the economic order quantity (EOQ) is very small. It often happens in practice that the economic order quantities turn out to be much higher than the replenishment order quantities used previously. In this case management are highly unlikely to permit immediate adoption of the use of EOQs because of the increase in stock capital required. In this situation, the possibility must be investigated of placing replenishment orders which are smaller than the EOQs. To this end it has been suggested that

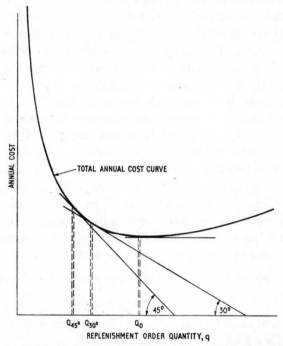

Fig. 3.5. Graphical interpretation of minimum economic order quantities

having differentiated the function representing annual inventory operating costs—Eqn. (3.7)—rather than equating the result with the true minimum, it is possible to find that order quantity which subtends an angle of, say either 30° or 45° with the horizontal axis by equating with $-1/\sqrt{3}$ and -1 respectively. These so called 'minimum economic order quantities' are shown in Fig. 3.5 and their values can be calculated using

$$Q_{30°} = \sqrt{\left[\frac{2\sqrt{3}C_oA}{\sqrt{3}C_h+2}\right]} \tag{3.10}$$

to find the MEOQ subtending an angle of 30° with the horizontal, or

$$Q_{45°} = \sqrt{\left[\frac{2C_oA}{C_h+2}\right]} \qquad (3.11)$$

for the MEOQ subtending an angle of 45°.

A limitation of the concept of minimum economic order quantities is that it depends on the units of cost employed, that is whether pounds or pence. This is because the scale of the ordinate axis directly influences the shape of the cost curve to which the tangents of 30° and 45° are hypothetically being drawn to evaluate $Q_{30°}$ and $Q_{45°}$ respectively. When using this technique, therefore, the units of cost should initially be chosen with great care. The smaller the unit the closer $Q_{45°}$, $Q_{30°}$ and Q_o will be to each other; the higher the unit of cost the greater will be their separation.

To illustrate how slight the increase in the total annual cost is when using correctly chosen minimum economic order quantities rather than the economic order quantity itself, let us again consider the data used previously but this time with some specification of costs.

As will be remembered, the following values of average demand, re-order level and average leadtime were used, namely

$$M = 300 \text{ units}, \quad \bar{D} = 50 \text{ units per week}, \quad L = 3 \text{ weeks}$$

Now consider in addition that the costs involved in placing a replenishment order C_o and the cost of holding one item of stock for a year C_h are £1·50 and 25p respectively.

All the variables used within the formulae quoted are now available with the exception of A which for a 50 week year can be evaluated as $50\bar{D} = 2\,500$ units sold per annum. Substituting these values in the relevant formula, Q_o, and $Q_{30°}$ and $Q_{45°}$ can then be found, and using these values as q in Eqn. (3.7), the total annual cost of using each such replenishment order size can be evaluated separately. The complete results of this analysis are shown in Table 3.6.

From this table it can be seen readily that for a substantial reduction of 17 units in the value of the EOQ from 173 to 156 units (a 10 per cent reduction) the total annual costs increase by only 40p (a 0·5 per cent rise) and for a further reduction of 10 units (a 5·75 per cent reduction)

Table 3.6 COMPARISON OF COSTS FOR DIFFERING REPLENISHMENT ORDER SIZES

Replenishment order size, units	$Q_0 = 173$	$Q_{30^\circ} = 156$	$Q_{45^\circ} = 146$
Annual holding costs	£59.00	£57.50	£55.50
Annual ordering costs	£21.60	£24.00	£25.75
Total annual costs	£80.60	£81.00	£81.25

the total annual cost increases by a further 25p (a 0·31 per cent rise). Below a replenishment order quantity of Q_{45°, the increase in total annual costs with decreasing order sizes becomes more rapid and it is, therefore, not feasible to operate below this point.

Effect of Price Reductions for Bulk Purchases

In the situation where a price reduction per item is offered by a supplier for purchases over and above a certain quantity, this effect of sudden price breaks in the material costs of stock items must be taken into account.

Where it is still assumed (in spite of price breaks) that the annual cost of holding a particular item is the same irrespective of its material cost, the situation in Fig. 3.4 still exists. To take advantage of the price breaks to reduce the overall material costs involved, however, the replenishment order size should be chosen as that which occurs just above a price break but nearest either the EOQ or MEOQ, whichever is being used as a guide. For instance, in the previous analysis if a unit price reduction were made for every additional 25 units purchased above 100, and the EOQ were being used as a guide, 175 units rather than 173 should be ordered; if Q_{30° then 150 units instead of 156.

For the situation in which it is assumed that holding costs are a proportion of an item's material and labour cost (i.e. $C_h = iC_m$), the holding cost curve becomes discontinuous with regard to replenishment order size. This feature is illustrated in Fig. 3.6 which is a graphical representation of holding costs in the situation where $i = 10$ per cent and the material price breaks for the item being considered are as in Table 3.7.

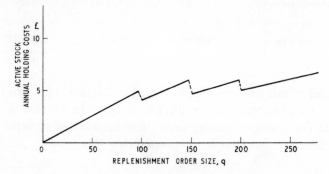

Fig. 3.6. Changes in holding costs due to price breaks

Table 3.7. TYPICAL PRICE LIST
WITH PRICE BREAKS

Quantity	Price per item, p
Up to 100	50
100–149	40
150–199	30
Above 200	25

When such a discontinuous holding cost is combined with a continuous ordering cost, obviously the resultant total cost will also be discontinuous and of the form shown in Fig. 3.7. It is evident that although the price breaks produce a sudden drop in the total cost it is possible to have lower total cost points which do not occur just after a price break. Therefore, in this situation the evaluated total cost curve must be examined before deciding on a replenishment order size.

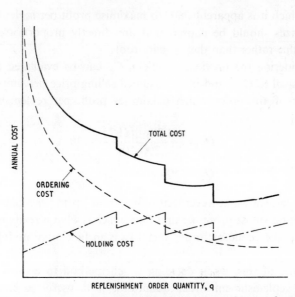

Fig. 3.7. Annual cost for proportional holding costs and imposed material price breaks

Maximising Profit rather than Minimising Costs

Eilon[1] has argued that rather than finding the replenishment order quantity that minimises the cost of ordering and holding stocks, a more realistic criterion would perhaps be that of maximising profit per replenishment. To evaluate the replenishment order size Q_p which maximises the gross profit per replenishment order, it is necessary to know the selling price per unit, C_a, which, therefore, produces a profit per unit of $C_a - C_m$, and it can be shown that the value of Q_p is given by

$$Q_p = \frac{C_a - C_m}{2C_o} Q_o^2 \qquad (3.12)$$

Substituting for Q_o in Eqn. (3.12) it can be shown that

$$Q_p = \frac{C_a - C_m}{C_h} A$$

from which it is apparent that, to maximise profit per replenishment, order sizes should be chosen that are directly proportional to the sales value rather than their square root.

Considering the previous problem, C_m can be evaluated as £1·25 being equal to C_h/i, and if the assumed selling price per unit is £1·30 the size of the order which maximises profit per replenishment is given by

$$Q_p = \frac{(£1·30)-(£1·25)}{2(£1·50)} 173^2$$

$$Q_p = 500 \text{ units}$$

Tate[6] has shown however that to maximise profit per replenishment does not maximise profit per unit time which is what is really required, and that the economic order quantity is in fact more useful in this respect.

In spite of this, when deciding which method to employ in evaluating replenishment order quantities, it is useful to know that investment in stocks can be reduced without substantially increasing the aggregate cost of holding and ordering, but that to maximise profit per replenishment order, a larger investment must be made as Q_p is in practice always greater than the economic order quantity. The criterion which any particular business might choose in selecting their replenishment order sizes will of course depend on the type of product range they sell, their management objectives and the market within which they operate.

Sensitivity of the Annual Inventory Operating Costs to Changes in the Annual Usage Rate when using the EOQ to Evaluate Replenishment Order Quantities

When using the EOQ as a guide to the size of replenishment quantities, it would be interesting to know what increase in the annual inventory operating cost of a stock item is likely to occur as a result of variables within the EOQ formula differing from what was originally expected. Of these variables the annual usage A, derived from some forecasting procedure, is the one most likely to be different from the actual value experienced. It can be shown that if the actual annual usage rate varies from that predicted by x per cent, then the ratio of the actual annual cost involved in controlling stocks, C^1, to that involved if the annual usage had been as predicted, C, is given by

$$\frac{C^1}{C} = \frac{1}{2}\left\{\sqrt{(1+x/100)} + \frac{1}{\sqrt{(1+x/100)}}\right\} \quad (3.13)$$

Values of the percentage increase in inventory operating costs incurred as a result of using the EOQ as computed with an annual usage figure which in retrospect proves to be in error from -50 up to $+150$ per cent are shown in Table 3.8.

Table 3.8. INCREASES IN INVENTORY OPERATING COSTS
DUE TO ERROR IN ESTIMATING ANNUAL USAGE

Percentage error in annual usage	Percentage increase in inventory operating costs using EOQ
-50	6·05
-40	3·28
-30	1·59
-20	0·62
-10	0·14
0	0·00
$+10$	0·11
$+20$	0·41
$+30$	0·86
$+40$	1·42
$+50$	2·06
$+75$	3·94
$+100$	6·06
$+125$	8·33
$+150$	10·68

It can be seen that if the actual annual usage is either half (-50 per cent) or double ($+100$ per cent) that predicted, then the annual inventory operating costs will be increased by about 6 per cent as a result of using the economic order quantity for calculating replenishments. It is then really a matter of subjective judgement as to whether one considers this cost increase to be large or small compared with the substantial error in predicting the annual usage; but at least this sensitivity analysis does provide a quantitative estimate of the cost increases likely to occur as a result of poor forecasting when using replenishments based on the economic order quantity.

Although economic order quantity theory is often criticised, it does provide a guide to the replenishment order sizes that should be used. The method at least gives a more consistently accurate criterion when considering replenishment of inventory items than does intuitive guesswork. References 4, 5, 6 and 7 should interest readers who may wish for further details and concepts of the theory of economic order quantities.

This chapter has considered the calculation of both the re-order level and replenishment order quantity completely in isolation. Chapter 4 discusses the joint calculation of these two quantities.

EXERCISES

1. For a leadtime of one week, what is the probability that demand during the leadtime will exceed ten units if the average demand per week is six units and is distributed as (a) a Poisson, or (b) an exponential distribution?

Answer. (a) 4·3 per cent (b) 21 per cent

2 (a). What service level is afforded by a re-order level of 200 when demand per week is distributed normally with a mean value of 40 and a standard deviation of 20, if the leadtime is fixed at 3 weeks?

(b). To what value does the service level slump if the leadtime begins to vary with an average value as before of 3 weeks but with now, a standard deviation of 1 week?

Answer. (a) 98·95 per cent (b) 97 per cent approximately

3 (a). What is the probability of running out of stock with a re-order level of 80 if demand is distributed approximately to an exponential

distribution with an average value of 10 and leadtimes of 2, 3 or 4 weeks have an equal probability of occurring?

(b). To what value does the probability of stockout rise if the actual effect of overshoot is taken into consideration?

Answer. (a) 7·1 per cent (b) 9·9 per cent for an overshoot average of 9·5

4 (a). Calculate the values of the various economic order quantities Q_o, $Q_{30°}$ and $Q_{45°}$ based on a pound cost unit, for the situation in which the annual turnover is 3 000 items, the cost of placing a replenishment order is £10 and the cost of holding an item of stock for a year is £1·50.

(b) If the profit per item of stock sold is 25p, what is the value of Q_p the maximum profit per replenishment batch?

Answer. (a) $Q_o = 200$ units, $Q_{30°} = 150$ units and $Q_{45°} = 131$ units
   (b) $Q_p = 500$ units

5. For the situation considered in Question 4, if the re-order level is 500 units and the average demand during the leadtime 350 units, what is (a) the total operating cost per year
   (b) the gross profit per year
   (c) the gross profit per replenishment

when using the replenishment order sizes of Q_o, $Q_{30°}$ and Q_p respectively?

Answer. (a) £525, £537 and £660
   (b) £225, £213 and £90
   (c) £15,   £10·65 and £15

6. What percentage increase in annual inventory operating costs would be expected if the annual usage figure used in evaluating the EOQ were found to be (a) 25 per cent low, or (b) 25 per cent high?

Answer. (a) 1·04 per cent
   (b) 0·62 per cent

REFERENCES

1. LEWIS, C. D., 'Generating a Continuous Trend Corrected, Exponentially Weighted Average on an Analogue Computer', *Opl Res. Q.*, **17**, No. 1, 77 (1966).
2. LAMPKIN, W., 'A Review of Inventory Control Theory', *The Production Engineer*, Vol 46, No. 2, p. 57, 1967.
3. WILSON, R. H., 'A Scientific Routine for Stock Control', *Harv. Bus. Rev.* XIII (1934–35).
4. BURBIDGE, J. L., 'The Case against the Economic Batch Quantity', *The Manager*, **32** (1964).
5. EILON, S., 'Dragons in Pursuit of the E.B.Q.', *Opl Res. Q.*, **15**, No. 4, 347 (1964).
6. TATE, T. B., 'In Defence of the Economic Batch Quantity', *Opl Res. Q.*, **15**, No. 4, 329 (1964).
7. EILON, S., *Elements of Production Planning and Control*, McMillan; New York, (1962).

CHAPTER 4

Re-order Level Policy: Joint Calculation of Re-order Levels and Replenishment Order Quantities

In Chapter 3, the calculations of both re-order levels and replenishment order quantities were dealt with in isolation. Many authors have noted, however, that for true optimum operation of a re-order level policy these two quantities must be calculated jointly. This is because the size of one quantity directly influences the size of the other in the overall re-order level inventory situation.

Obviously a joint calculation procedure will be more complicated and one must, therefore, decide whether this additional computational effort is really providing an overall cost saving to the business. Likewise, the inclusion of this chapter on joint calculation is not a condemnation of all that was included in Chapter 3 but merely indicates the progress that has been made in this field. For instance, criticism of the economic order quantity approach is not levelled at the method itself but at the assumptions that have to be made for the method to be valid. If in practice these assumptions just happen to exist, then there is no earthly reason why such an approach should not be used. It is the misapplication of the basic formulae to situations for which the assumptions made are not valid that bring such methods into disrepute.

JOINT CALCULATION OF RE-ORDER LEVELS AND REPLENISHMENT ORDER SIZES

Several complicated mathematical models have been developed for the joint calculation of re-order levels and replenishment order quantities but most are either too complex mathematically or subject to special conditions which render their general application impossible.

A recent method proposed by Tate[1] makes certain reasonable approximations, and by so doing achieves two relatively simple formulae for the evaluation of joint re-order levels and replenishment order quantities. In the author's opinion, this method has much to recommend it as it appears to be a happy compromise between on the one hand an attempt to find too accurate an answer in what is basi-

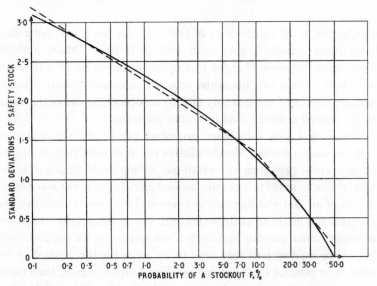

Fig. 4.1. Probability of a stockout for a given standard deviations of safety stock, with two linear approximations

$$\log_e F = 5.65 - 2.49k, \quad 0.1 \leqslant F \leqslant 10$$
$$\log_e F = 4.08 - 1.32k, \quad 10.0 \leqslant F \leqslant 50$$

cally an imprecise situation, and on the other, a model so simple as to be inapplicable for most practical situations.

Tate's initial assumptions are that demand per unit time is distributed normally, leadtimes are reasonably constant and the resultant probability F of a stockout occurring, given a safety stock of k standard deviations of demand during the leadtime, is described with a maximum error of only 3 per cent by two linear logarithmic approximations (see Fig. 4.1) such that

i.e.
$$\log_e F = a - bk \tag{4.1}$$
$$F = e^{a-bk} \tag{4.2}$$

where $a = 5\cdot65$ and $b = 2\cdot49$ for $1\cdot3 \leqslant k \leqslant 3\cdot2$ $(0\cdot1\% \leqslant F \leqslant 10\%)$

$a = 4\cdot08$ and $b = 1\cdot32$ for $0 \leqslant k \leqslant 1\cdot3$ $(10\% \leqslant F \leqslant 50\%)$

The total annual cost C (now including a stockout term) can then be evaluated as follows:

C = number of stockouts per year $\times$ cost of an individual stockout
  + number of replenishment orders placed $\times$ cost of placing an order
  + $\frac{1}{2}$ average replenishment quantity $\times$ unit cost of holding
  + safety stock $\times$ unit cost of holding

Thus

$$C = \frac{AC_s\, e^{a-bk}}{100q} + \frac{AC_o}{q} + \frac{qC_h}{2} + k\sigma_d\sqrt{\overline{L}C_h} \tag{4.3}$$

The values of k^* and q^* that minimise C are then found by differentiating C partially with respect to both k and q and setting these partial derivatives $\partial C/\partial k$ and $\partial C/\partial q$ simultaneously to zero.

Hence
$$\frac{-bAC_s\, e^{a-bk^*}}{100q^*} + \sigma_d\sqrt{\overline{L}C_h} = 0$$

and
$$\frac{-AC_s\, e^{a-bk^*}}{100q^{*2}} - \frac{AC_o}{q^{*2}} + \frac{C_h}{2} = 0$$

from which:

$$q^* = \frac{\sigma_d\sqrt{L}}{b} + \sqrt{\left[\frac{\sigma_d^2\overline{L}}{b^2} + \frac{2AC_o}{C_h}\right]} \tag{4.4}$$

It is interesting to note that the size of the replenishment order quantity is not only always higher than the economic order quantity Q_q for all practical situations but is also independent of C_s the cost of stockout.

The corresponding number of standard deviations of demand during the leadtime k^*, required as safety stock for use in conjunction with q^* the replenishment order quantity calculated above is given by

$$k^* = \frac{1}{b} \left[a - \frac{\log_e 100\, \sigma_d \sqrt{\bar{L} C_h q^*}}{b C_s A} \right] \qquad (4.5)$$

Hence for $1 \cdot 3 \leqslant k \leqslant 3 \cdot 2$ $(0 \cdot 1\% \leqslant F \leqslant 10\%)$

$$k^* = \frac{1}{2 \cdot 49} \left[5 \cdot 65 - \frac{\log_e 100\, \sigma_d \sqrt{\bar{L} C_h q^*}}{2 \cdot 49 C_s A} \right]$$

and for $0 \leqslant k \leqslant 1 \cdot 3$ $(10\% \leqslant F \leqslant 50\%)$

$$k^* = \frac{1}{1 \cdot 32} \left[4 \cdot 08 - \frac{\log_e 100\, \sigma_d \sqrt{\bar{L} C_h q^*}}{1 \cdot 32 C_s A} \right]$$

These two formulae for k^* produce overlapping solutions in the region $0 \cdot 13 < \dfrac{q^* \sigma_d \sqrt{\bar{L} C_h}}{C_s A} < 0 \cdot 25$, but it can be shown that the lower value of k^* provides the optimal solution when $q^* \sigma_d \sqrt{\bar{L} C_h}/C_s A$ is greater than $0 \cdot 19$. This enables a graph to be plotted on logarithmic paper from which k^* can be found directly, once having evaluated $q^* \sigma_d \sqrt{\bar{L} C_h}/C_s A$ (see Fig. 4.2).

Tate points out that the calculation of the replenishment order quantity q^* using Eqn. (4.4), leads to substantial economies in inventory operating costs only if the standard deviation of demand during the leadtime is greater in value than the economic order quantity Q_o. If this standard deviation of demand during the leadtime is not greater than Q_o, no great loss will be incurred by calculating Q_o, using Eqn. (3.11) and then reading off from Fig. 4.2 the corresponding value of k^* required having evaluated in this case

$$\frac{Q_o \sigma_d \sqrt{\bar{L} C_h}}{C_s A}$$

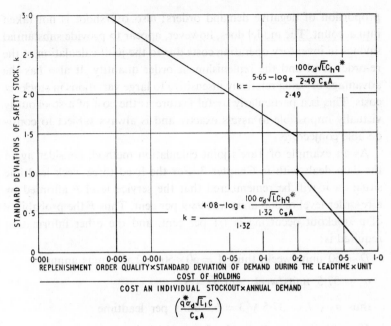

Fig. 4.2. Graph for safety stock

Tables showing the calculation of the optimum replenishment order size q^* and the economic order quantity Q_o, and indicating the ratio of their values for typical inventory situations are given as Table 4.1.

Having found the value of k^*, the re-order level required can obviously be found using

$$M = \bar{D}\bar{L} + k^*\sigma_d\sqrt{\bar{L}} \tag{4.6}$$

Where it cannot be assumed that the leadtime is constant, an attempt should be made to evaluate the standard deviation of demand during the leadtime as either $\sqrt{(\bar{L}\sigma_d^2 + \bar{D}^2\sigma_l^2)}$ or from 1·1 to 1·4 times the standard deviation of demand during an *average* leadtime. This value would then be substituted for $\sigma_d\sqrt{\bar{L}}$ in the formulae derived for Tate's method of joint calculation.

Tate's model has certain limitations insofar that once more the assumption of normally distributed demand presupposes a small proportion of negative demand orders; also overshoot is not taken into account. The model does, however, appear to provide substantial savings in inventory operating costs due to the joint calculation of the re-order level and the replenishment order quantity. It also has the advantage of being relatively insensitive to large variations in stockout costs. This is a particularly useful feature as the cost of a stockout is virtually impossible to assess exactly and is always subject to considerable conjecture.

As an example of Tate's joint calculation method, consider again the data dealt with in Chapter 3. For the fixed three week leadtime situation it will be remembered that the service level P afforded by a re-order level of 300 units was 98·9 per cent. Thus F the probability of a stockout occurring is 1·1 per cent, and the other information required is:

$\bar{D} = 50$ units/week, thus $A = 50 \times 50 = 2\,500$ units/annum

$\sigma_d = 37 \cdot 5$ units/week and $\bar{L} = 3$,

thus $\sigma_d \sqrt{\bar{L}} = 37 \cdot 5 \sqrt{3} = 65$ units per leadtime

$C_o = £1.50$ and $C_h = 25$p from which it was shown $Q_o = 173$ units.

Because the standard deviation of demand during the leadtime (65) is less than the economic order quantity (173), by Tate's ruling there is no need to calculate q^* the optimum order quantity. Thus k^* the number of standard deviations of demand during the leadtime required as safety stock can be read directly from Fig. 4.2 once $\dfrac{Q_o \sigma_d \sqrt{\bar{L} C_h}}{C_s A}$ has been evaluated. So far, the cost of an individual stockout C_s has not been considered so let us here assume a figure of £10 as being reasonable. Thus

$$\frac{Q_o \sigma_d \sqrt{\bar{L} C_h}/C_s A}{C_s A} = \frac{173 \times 65 \times (25\text{p})}{(£10) \times 2 \cdot 500} = 0 \cdot 112$$

and this produces a value of $k^* = 1 \cdot 535$ from Fig. 4.2.

Thus the re-order level is given by

$$M = DL + k^* \sigma_d \sqrt{\bar{L}} = 50 \times 3 + 1 \cdot 535 \times 65 = 250$$

This re-order level of 250 evaluated using the joint calculation method is thus 50 units less than that calculated to achieve the same service level using the independent calculation method, and this difference can be attributed to the inclusion within the joint calculation method of a consideration of the stockout cost which was not incorporated previously.

JOINT CALCULATION OF RE-ORDER LEVELS AND REPLENISHMENT ORDER SIZES FOR SLOW MOVING PARTS

It has been explained that the concept of a customer 'service level' being afforded by a re-order level of a specified value does not indicate the frequency or duration of stockouts in a re-order level system, and also does not indicate the proportion of demand orders not fulfilled immediately ex-stock as a result of those stockouts occurring. Lampkin and Flowerdew[2,3] have proposed that the two criteria of either *customer demands met immediately ex-stock* or *items months of stock shortage per annum* are more realistic to the inventory situation involving slow moving items such as spare parts. These criteria are also, it is claimed, more comprehensible to management, who are eventually the sole arbiters of what a company's inventory stock-holding policy should be.

The first of these criteria is very useful in a situation where one is supplying goods, in competition with others, direct to a customer and where any delay in supplying customers' demand orders indicates the proportion of customer disappointments.

The second criterion is particularly applicable in the inventory situation involving the supply of spare parts, where the delay involved in supplying a part to a customer increases his costs of operating by causing a production delay.

It can be shown that for the situation where overshoot can be ignored and backordering is permitted, $G(M, Q)$, the expected proportion of demands met immediately ex-stock when using a re-order level of M and a replenishment order quantity Q, is given by

$$G(M, Q) = \sum_{r=0}^{r=M} p_{\bar{L}}(r) + \frac{1}{Q} \sum_{r=M+1}^{r=M+Q} (M+Q-r)\, p_{\bar{L}}(r) \qquad (4.7)$$

where $p_{\bar{L}}(r)$ denotes the probability of r demands in a leadtime $\bar{L}$.

Similarly, the average number of item months of shortage per annum, $B(M, Q)$, is

$$B(M, Q) = 12\left[\sum_{r=0}^{r=M} \left(M + \frac{Q+1}{2} - r\right) p_{\bar{L}}(r) \right.$$

$$+ \frac{1}{2Q} \sum_{r=M+1}^{r=M+Q} (M+Q+1-r)(M+Q-r)\, p_{\bar{L}}(r)$$

$$\left. - \left(M + \frac{Q+1}{2} - \bar{D}\bar{L}\right) \right] \qquad (4.8)$$

Although these formulae look at first sight rather complicated they contain only single summations, and values can be readily computed on a computer. An example of manual calculation of $G(M, Q)$ and $B(M, Q)$ is given, however, to illustrate the method.

Suppose the value and probability of demand per week to be as shown in columns A and B of Table 4.2, then the remaining columns indicate the values required for the computation of $G(M, Q)$ and $B(M, Q)$ over the relevant ranges of r. These can be added and entered as summed values in the formulae, and values for $G(M, Q)$ and $B(M, Q)$ calculated as 0·9 and 1·44 respectively.

The value of $G(M, Q)$ of 0·9 indicates, that with a re-order level of 8 and a replenishment order size of 12, a re-order level policy subjected to the demand distribution indicated will ensure that 90 per cent of all demand orders will be fulfilled immediately ex-stock, and the remaining 10 per cent will be delayed.

A value of $B(M, Q)$ of 1·44 item months stock shortage per annum, indicates that for approximately 1·5 months of every year *one* item of stock will be on shortage.

Where it is possible to assess the cost per unmet demand, it can be shown that to minimise the average annual inventory costs the re-order level should be chosen such that the service level just exceeds

Table 4.2. Data and Summation of values required for $G(M, Q)$* and $B(M, Q)$†

Demand week A	Probability of occurrence, % B	Demand during leadtime, r	$p_L(r)$	$\sum_{r=0}^{8} p_{\bar{L}}(r)$	$\sum_{r=9}^{20}\left(\frac{M+Q-r}{Q}\right) \times p_{\bar{L}}(r)$	$\sum_{r=0}^{8}\left(M+\frac{Q+1}{2}-r\right) \times p_{\bar{L}}(r)$	$\sum_{r=9}^{20}\left(\frac{(M+Q+1-r)(M+Q-r)}{2Q}\right) \times p_{\bar{L}}(r)$
4	10	4	0·1	0·1	—	10·5 × 0·1 = 1·05	—
6	20	6	0·2	0·2	—	8·5 × 0·2 = 1·70	—
8	30	8	0·3	0·3	—	6·5 × 0·3 = 1·95	—
10	20	10	0·2	—	$\frac{10}{12} \times 0·2 = 0·167$	—	$\frac{11 \times 10}{24} \times 0·2 = 0·92$
12	20	12	0·2	—	$\frac{8}{12} \times 0·2 = 0·133$	—	$\frac{9 \times 8}{24} \times 0·2 = 0·60$
				0·6	0·300	4·70	1·52

$$* \ G(M, Q) = \sum_{r=0}^{8} p_L(r) + \frac{1}{Q}\sum_{r=9}^{20}(M+Q-r)p_L(r) = 0·6 + 0·300 = 0·9$$

$$† \ B(M, Q) = 12\left[\sum_{r=0}^{8}(M+Q+1-r)(M+Q-r)p_L(r) + \frac{1}{2Q}\sum_{r=9}^{20}(M+Q+1-r)(M+Q-r)p_L(r) - \left(M + \frac{(Q+1)}{2} - \bar{D}L\right)\right]$$
$$= 12[4·70 + 1·52 - 6·1] \text{ (with } \bar{D} = 8·4) = 1·44$$

a value of $100(1-C_miQ/AY)$, where Y denotes the cost per unmet demand. Applying this to the previously considered data for which demand per unit time was distributed normally with a mean value of 50 units per week and a standard deviation of 37·5, and where Q_o was calculated as 173 units, $i = 10$ per cent and $C_m = 25\text{p}$, the service levels required and, therefore, the re-order levels for differing costs of unmet demand are indicated in Table 4.3.

Table 4.3. RE-ORDER LEVELS REQUIRED TO MINIMISE OPERATING COST FOR COSTS OF UNMET DEMANDS

Cost of unmet demand, Y	$(1-C_miQ/SR)$	Service level, %	Normal deviate, k	Re-order level
25p	0·9711	97·11	1·900	273
50p	0·9856	98·56	2·185	292
£1	0·9928	99·28	2·445	309
£1·50	0·9952	99·52	2·587	318

Where the cost per item month of stock shortage is relevant, and Z denotes that cost, then the rule to decide the value for M is to choose the highest value of M for which the following inequality is valid:

$$G(M, Q) < \frac{Z}{12C_mi+Z} \qquad (4.9)$$

Although in theory, to find the absolute minimum average operating costs it is necessary to use a lengthy computer routine to find the best combination of M and Q, in practice the increased costs involved in using Q_o or $Q_{30°}$ and then evaluating M are not very high and the computational procedure is that much simplified.

EXERCISES

1. Given that customer demand is distributed normally with a mean value of 100 units/month and a standard deviation of 60 units/month, that all replenishment orders are delayed by two months and that $C_o/C_h = 2·5$, is it necessary to calculate q^* using Tate's method of joint evaluation?

Answer. Yes as $Q_o = 77 \cdot 2$ units and $\sigma_d \sqrt{\bar{L}} = 84 \cdot 5$ units.

2. Calculate both the replenishment order size and the re-order level required to minimise inventory operating costs for the situation described in Question 1 if $C_s/C_h = 96$. What customer service level does this provide?

Answer. $q^* = 118$ units, $ROL = 349$ units and $P = 96 \cdot 2$ per cent as $k^* = 1 \cdot 77$

3. If it were known in the above situation that the cost of a stockout had altered and by simulation it was found that this new situation was optimised by operating at a 98 per cent service level but with the same replenishment order size, what is the new assumed ratio of C_s/C_h?

Answer. 173

4. For the situation described in Question 3, given that the ratio of holding cost and cost of placing a replenishment order still remain as in Question 1; if it cost £1·50 to place an order what is the assumed cost of stockout?

Answer. £10·50

5. If the probability of demand during the leadtime is distributed as indicated, what is

(a) the proportion of demands that will on average be met directly ex-stock and

(b) the average number of item months of shortage, where $M = 300$, $Q = 150$, $\bar{D} = 100$ and $\bar{L} = 2 \cdot 5$?

Demand during leadtime	Probability, %
150	15
200	20
250	30
300	20
350	15

Answer. a. 95 per cent

  b. 0·18 item months

REFERENCES

1. TATE, T. B., 'When the EBQ is too small ...' private communication (1968).
2. LAMPKIN, W. and FLOWERDEW, A. D. J., 'Computation of Re-order Levels and Quantities for a Re-order Level Stock System', *Opl Res. Q.*, **14**, No. 3, 263 (1968).
3. LAMPKIN, W. 'A Review of Inventory Control Theory', *Prod. Engr.*, **46**, No. 2, 57 (1967).

Cyclical Policies: Re-order Cycle Policy, Re-order Level Policy Subject to Periodic Review, (s, S) Policy

THE RE-ORDER CYCLE POLICY

Because the re-order cycle policy is a time based inventory system, the value of the service level achieved when operating this policy has much more relevance than when considering the re-order level policy. This is because with the review time being fixed, the *frequency* of stockouts can be directly related to the *probability* of a stockout occurring. For instance, it follows that if a re-order cycle policy has a review period of one month and a service level of 91·6 per cent (i.e. 11/12), the frequency of stockouts per year will, on average, be one.

For the re-order cycle policy there are only two parameters whose values must be chosen. These are S the maximum fixed inventory level from which all replenishment orders are calculated and R the policy's review period.

It is possible to find the so called economic review period (ERP) if one is prepared again to consider the minimisation of the annual cost of acquiring and holding stock as a reasonably valid criterion.

This annual cost C can then be defined as

C = Average inventory held × unit cost of holding + number of replenishment orders placed × cost of placing an order

Thus if m reviews are made per annum, C is given by

$$C = \frac{AC_h}{2m} + mC_o \qquad (5.1)$$

and by differentiating with respect to m and equating to zero we can obtain m as

$$m = \sqrt{\frac{AC_h}{2C_o}} \qquad (5.2)$$

Knowing how many reviews are made per year it is then a relatively simple matter to evaluate the economic review period.

In practice, however, the review period tends to be chosen by such factors as the number of clerks available to inspect stock records regularly, or is fixed to correspond to some convenient standard unit of time such as a week or a month. In this situation with the review period known, only the value of S to be used within the re-order cycle policy need be determined.

When examining in detail inventory balances for a typical re-order cycle policy (Fig. 5.1) after placing a particular replenishment order, it is evident that the only decision affecting whether or not a stockout occurs subsequent to the receipt of that replenishment order, is the placing of the next replenishment order. As this is placed at the next review period and will also be subject to a leadtime delay, it is apparent that the period of uncertainty due to the placing of *any* particular replenishment order is equal to its associated leadtime plus the preceding review period. Thus one can consider the re-order cycle policy to be continuously at risk, and in this situation S becomes analogous to M the re-order level where the period of risk is now $(R+\bar{L})$ rather than just $\bar{L}$ as in the case of the re-order level policy. Thus by replacing $(R+\bar{L})$ for $\bar{L}$ and S for M in the familiar re-order level formula, for the fixed leadtime situation, S is evaluated when demand is normal as

$$S = \bar{D}(R+\bar{L}) + k\sigma_d \sqrt{(R+\bar{L})} \qquad (5.3)$$

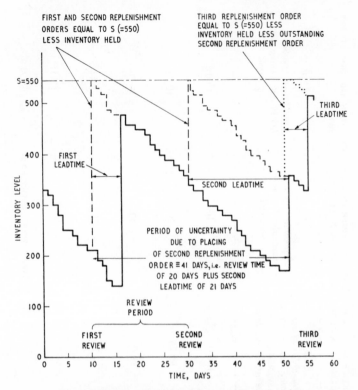

Fig. 5.1. Inventory balances for a re-order cycle policy

If the value of k derived from equation (5.2) indicates a service level or P per cent, it follows that if the review time R is expressed in weeks, the annual frequency of stockout f is given by

$$f = \frac{100 - P}{2R} \tag{5.4}$$

for a 50 week year.

When it cannot be assumed that the leadtime is reasonably constant, S can be determined by using either the iterative calculation technique, or a simulation method (see Chapter 10, p. 164). An example of the iterative technique as applied to a re-order cycle policy is illustrated in Table 5.1. For this example the review period is 4 weeks and the

Table 5.1. ITERATIVE METHOD OF CALCULATING SERVICE LEVELS FOR A 4 WEEK RE-ORDER CYCLE POLICY WHEN THE DEMAND PER UNIT TIME IS DISTRIBUTED NORMALLY AND THE DISTRIBUTION OF LEADTIMES IS KNOWN

Lead-time	Leadtime plus review period $R(=4)$	Value of k when $S=550$	A Probability of not-running out of stock corresponding to the value of k calculated %	B Probability of this particular leadtime occurring %	$A \times B$ Conditional probability of not running out of stock %
1	5	$\dfrac{550-250}{37 \cdot 5\sqrt{5}} = 3 \cdot 58$	100·0	10	10·0
2	6	$\dfrac{550-300}{37 \cdot 5\sqrt{6}} = 2 \cdot 72$	99·75	20	19·94
3	7	$\dfrac{550-350}{37 \cdot 5\sqrt{7}} = 2 \cdot 05$	98·0	40	39·20
4	8	$\dfrac{550-400}{37 \cdot 5\sqrt{8}} = 1 \cdot 42$	92·2	20	18·44
5	9	$\dfrac{500-450}{37 \cdot 5\sqrt{9}} = 0 \cdot 89$	81·3	10	8·13
				Total overall service level	95·71

value of S is 550 units; the demand and leadtime data is the same as considered for the re-order level policy in Chapter 3. This iterative re-order cycle calculation indicates that a policy of this type with a 4 week review period and a value of S of 550 units provides a service level of 95·71 per cent and from this value the annual frequency of stockouts f is given by

$$f = \frac{100 - 95\cdot71}{2\times4} \div \frac{1}{2}$$

Thus, on average when operating this re-order cycle policy a stockout is likely to occur once every two years.

It should be noted that when the leadtime becomes longer than the review period for the re-order cycle policy, the replenishment order size is as usual calculated as S less the inventory on-hand but in this situation the inventory on-hand is equal to the inventory held *plus* the outstanding replenishment order which has still to be received (again refer to Fig. 5.1).

THE RE-ORDER LEVEL POLICY SUBJECT TO PERIODIC REVIEWS

Although the re-order level policy with periodic reviews is a time based inventory system, it is not possible to relate the frequency of stockouts with their probability of occurring as was possible with the re-order cycle policy. This is because although reviews do occur regularly, it does not follow that orders for replenishment are also placed regularly as such orders are not necessarily placed at every review. A frequency of stockout calculated using Eqn. (5.4) would indicate the maximum frequency of stockouts but this could be well above the actual frequency.

Referring to Fig. 5.2 it can be seen that with a periodic review system superimposed on a re-order level policy, the re-order level can be broken exactly at the same time as a review takes place; in which event there is no delay in placing the replenishment order. At the other extreme, however, the re-order level can be broken imme-

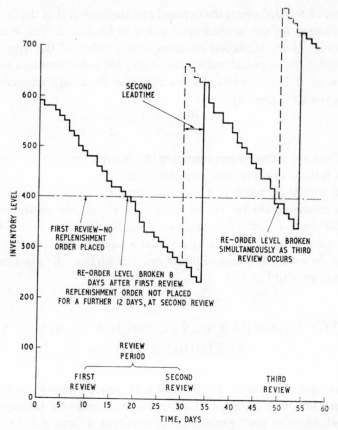

Fig. 5.2. Inventory balances for a re-order level policy subject to periodic reviews

diately after a review has taken place and a replenishment order will then not be placed until the next review occurs. On average, it can be estimated approximately that a replenishment order will be placed after a delay equal to half the review period and thus the value of the re-order level required to provide a certain level of service can be calculated using the traditional re-order level formula but with $(R/2+\bar{L})$ replacing $\bar{L}$, hence:

$$M = \bar{D}(R/2+\bar{L})+k\sigma_d\sqrt{(R/2+\bar{L})} \qquad (5.5)$$

for the fixed leadtime situation.

For the variable leadtime situation, as with all other policies, values can be found using either simulation techniques or an iterative calculation procedure.

An example of this iterative calculation procedure, using again the same demand data as considered previously but this time considering a re-order level policy subject to review every four weeks and operating with a re-order level of 400 units, is shown in Table 5.2. It is interesting to note from this calculation that when both a re-order level policy without periodic reviews (Chapter 3) and a re-order level policy subject to a four weekly review are both involved with the same demand and leadtime situation, the policy subject to review requires a re-order level of 400 units to provide a service level of 92·6 per cent, whereas the policy with no review system superimposed could provide a comparable service level (i.e. 95·36 per cent) with a re-order level of only 300 units. Thus it can be seen that the savings involved in dropping continuous monitoring and adopting a periodic review system have been gained at the expense of having to raise the re-order level by about 100 units to maintain a similar level of service.

A re-order level policy subject to very frequent review tends to behave more as a re-order level policy than as a re-order cycle policy because the breaking of the re-order level is the major factor governing the placing of further replenishment orders. Conversely, when review periods are relatively long this same policy tends to act more as a re-order cycle policy because the re-order level here is invariably broken at review and, therefore, replenishment orders are placed at nearly every review. There is obviously no point in operating the re-order level policy with periodic reviews at either of these two extremes as it then in no way improves the control of the stock situation compared with the original policies. Ideally periodic reviews should occur frequently enough that the actual time between placing replenishment orders is not always the same, and varies by about 1 to 3 review periods.

Table 5.2. Iterative method of calculating service levels for the re-order level policy subject to periodic review when the demand per unit time is distributed normally, and the distribution of leadtimes is known

Lead-time	Leadtime plus half the review period $R(=4)$	Value of k when $M = 400$	A Probability of not running out of stock corresponding to the value of k calculated %	B Probability of this particular leadtime occurring %	$A \times B$ Conditional probability of not running out of stock %
1	3	$\dfrac{400-150}{37 \cdot 5\sqrt{3}} = 3 \cdot 85$	100·0	10·0	10·0
2	4	$\dfrac{400-200}{37 \cdot 5\sqrt{4}} = 2 \cdot 66$	99·6	20·0	19·92
3	5	$\dfrac{400-250}{37 \cdot 5\sqrt{5}} = 1 \cdot 79$	96·3	40·0	38·52
4	6	$\dfrac{400-300}{37 \cdot 5\sqrt{6}} = 1 \cdot 09$	86·2	20·0	17·24
5	7	$\dfrac{400-350}{37 \cdot 5\sqrt{7}} = 0 \cdot 50$	69·2	10·0	6·92
				Total overall service level	92·60

THE (*s*, *S*) POLICY

Because the (*s*, *S*) policy has three adjustable control parameters, namely *s*, *S* and the review period *R*, the relationship between these parameters for optimum cost operation in even the most simple demand and leadtime situations tends to be very complicated mathematically. Arrow *et al.*[1, 2] have considered the optimal character of the (*s*, *S*) policy subject to fixed a cost of ordering and constant leadtimes and after lengthy mathematical analysis concluded that for optimal operation, the parameters *s* and *S* were related by two complex simultaneous integral equations. A less mathematical approach was shown by Alfandary-Alexander[3] in his extensive digital simulation of inventory policy situations. In this study Alfandary–Alexander was mainly concerned with the degree to which customer demand was satisfied, and he found that except for very low *s* cases, the fraction of lost sales was not too sensitive to changes in *S*. However, with *S* kept constant, relatively small variations in the level of *s* induced large improvements in the fraction of satisfied customer demand.

As has already been noted, an exact solution to the relationship of the various control parameters of an (*s*, *S*) policy for optimal cost operation is most complex mathematically. However, if one is prepared to accept that the average replenishment order size is reasonably well estimated as the difference between *S* and *s* (which represents the minimum possible replenishment order size) plus one-half the average expected usage during the review period (Magee[4] p. 85), this can then be equated with the economic order quantity for minimum cost inventory operation.

Thus,

$$Q_o = \sqrt{\frac{2AC_o}{C_h}} = S - s + \frac{A}{2} \times \frac{R}{50} \qquad (5.6)$$

where *R* is the review period expressed in weeks.

By transposing, *S* can be evaluated in terms of *s* and *R* (Eqn. (5.7)), and as in practice *R* is usually chosen to be some convenient unit of time, *s* and *S* then become directly related.

Thus,

$$S = \sqrt{\frac{2AC_o}{C_h} - s + \frac{AR}{100}} \qquad (5.7)$$

This method of choosing S and s given the value for R, is of course only very approximate as no direct consideration has been given to the proportion of replenishment orders which are placed at review.

From this discussion it is apparent that the author is not in a position to develop further equations describing the interrelationship of the control parameters of the (s, S) policy whose complexity is in general keeping with this book. However, because the (s, S) policy does demonstrate certain optimal characteristics and in many situations can operate an inventory system more economically than either the re-order level or re-order cycle policies, it definitely cannot be ignored altogether. Because of this, some of the results obtained by the author in his simulation of the (s, S) policy will be discussed in some detail in the hope that the results presented will be of some use to readers who themselves wish to investigate the use of the (s, S) policy. Conclusions drawn from this work must necessarily be regarded as having been developed from fairly limited evidence though they are substantiated by other workers (such as Alfandary-Alexander) in the field. Nevertheless, it is hoped that the suggestions made will at least help the reader to recognise those characteristics of the (s, S) policy which are likely to be observed when the policy is operating somewhere near the optimal condition for minimum overall inventory operating costs.

In the work discussed here (Lewis[5]) a series of simulation runs was performed and the total cost of operating the (s, S) policy was evaluated for a range of assumed holding, ordering and stockout costs. The series of simulation runs was split into two main sections within which:

(a) S was kept constant and s varied for optimal performance,

(b) s was kept constant and S varied for optimal performance.

These optimal costs of operation of the (s, S) policy were then compared with the *equivalent* re-order level and re-order cycle policies operating under the same demand and leadtime conditions. These equivalent policies were defined as:

EQUIVALENT RE-ORDER LEVEL POLICY

That re-order level policy (ROL) operating with a re-order level equal to s whose replenishment orders were computed on the same basis as those for the (s, S) policy, and also with the same value of S operating within that (s, S) policy with whose performance it was being compared. Such a policy is not a true re-order level policy in-so-far that replenishment order sizes are not fixed, but this policy was thought to be the most appropriate for direct comparison purposes.

EQUIVALENT RE-ORDER CYCLE POLICY

That re-order cycle policy (ROC) with the same review period and whose replenishment order quantities were computed with the corresponding value of S operating within the (s, S) policy.

Graphs showing the inventory operating costs evaluated by the simulation runs for these two policies and the minimum cost (s, S) policy subject to condition i or ii are shown as Figs. 5.3(a) and 5.3(b).

For case i, where s only was varied, it can be seen (Fig. 5.3(a)) that for short review periods the cost of operating the (s, S) policy was similar to that for operating the equivalent re-order level policy. As the review periods lengthen, however, the cost involved in operating the (s, S) policy became increasingly similar to that involved in operating the equivalent re-order cycle policy, until, with very long review periods it was found that the optimal (s, S) policy was that in which replenishment orders were placed at every review. In this condition the (s, S) policy was operating exactly as the equivalent re-order cycle policy, and the costs involved with both policies were therefore the same. These results indicate the ability of the optimal (s, S) policy under certain demand situations to 'bridge the gap' between the low cost characteristics of the re-order level policy when reviews for the (s, S) policy are frequent and the corresponding low operating costs of the re-order cycle policy when reviews for the (s, S) policy are made less frequently.

It is interesting to note (Fig. 5.3(b)) that for case ii, where only S was varied, the costs involved in operating the minimum cost (s, S) policy were always lower than either of the equivalent policies.

From the above observations it is apparent that if one can adjust the parameters of the (s, S) policy so that it operates optimally or nearly so, the chances are that the inventory operating costs involved will be less than those of either the optimal re-order level or re-order

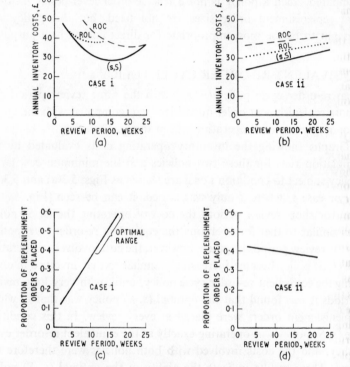

Fig. 5.3. Characteristics of the optimal (s, S) policy

cycle policies. As has already been stated, it is not within the mathematical scope of this book to define how the parameters of the (s, S) policy can be evaluated for such optimal operation, but other findings from the series of simulation runs described do give an indication of when the (s, S) policy is likely to be operating somewhere near the optimal minimum cost condition.

One such parameter derived from the simulation runs which appeared to be useful in deciding when this optimal operation was likely to be in evidence, was the proportion of replenishment orders placed. This is obviously defined as the number of replenishment orders actually placed divided by the number of review periods occurring in the same time period.

It is apparent that as the proportion of replenishment orders placed at review approaches a value of 1, the (s, S) policy is acting as a pure re-order cycle policy with a replenishment being placed at every review. Also when this value tends towards zero it is evident that the (s, S) is beginning to behave more in the manner of a re-order level policy.

For case i, where S was maintained constant and s allowed to vary (Fig. 5.3(c)) it can be seen that the cost operating advantages are most evident when the value of the proportion of replenishment orders placed lies in the range 0·4 to 0·6. For case ii, where s was maintained constant and S allowed to vary (Fig. 5.3(d)) the value of the proportion of replenishment orders placed remained fairly constant at a value of 0·4. From this evidence therefore, for this particular demand and leadtime situation, it would appear that using a criterion of a value of the proportion of replenishment orders placed as being between say 0·4 and 0·6 indicates when an (s, S) policy is likely to be operating in a manner producing lower operating costs than an equivalent re-order level or re-order cycle policy. In practice this means that on average a replenishment order should be placed at about every second review with occasional replenishments occurring at either successive or at third or fourth reviews.

In conclusion it can be seen that the (s, S) policy has certain operating cost advantages over the other two major policies. As a rough guide, the specific results found here would appear to indicate that these advantages are likely to be gained if the proportion of replenishments at review lies between 0·4 and 0·6 in the general inventory situation. If the (s, S) policy is being installed as a replacement for either a re-order level or re-order cycle policy which has been operating reasonably successfully, the value of the re-order level should be made equal to s and the review period and S varied to obtain the correct proportion in the former case, and the review period and S kept the same and s varied for the latter case. In general the (s, S) policy is more sensitive to changes in s than changes in S.

EXERCISES

1. Given that customer demand is distributed normally with an average value of 5 units/week and a standard deviation of 2 units/week, what is the length of the economic review period (to the nearest week) if the ratio of the unit cost of holding to the cost of placing a replenishment order is 1 : 5? If reviews are made in accordance with the ERP, with what value of S should replenishment orders be calculated if all such orders are fulfilled after a three week delay, and it is also required to provide a 95 per cent customer service level?

Answer. 10 weeks, and 77 units approximately

2. For the previous example, what is the average annual frequency of stockouts occurring?

Answer. 0·25 for a 50 week year

3. If the demand situation described in Question 1 were controlled by a re-order level policy subject to monthly reviews (i.e. every four weeks), what re-order level would be required to achieve the same level of customer service?

Answer. 32·4 units

4. What drop in customer service level is likely to occur in changing from a re-order cycle inventory policy with $S = 1\,400$ and two month reviews to a re-order level policy with quarterly reviews and a re-order level of 1 000 units? Assume one is dealing with a normally distributed demand of 100 units average and a standard deviation of 60 units. Assume also that all replenishment orders are delayed for a fortnight.

Answer. 10 per cent, that is, from 98·3 to 88·3 per cent

5. If the inventory policy used to cope with the demand situation described in Question 1 is of the (s, S) variety, what is the relationship between S and s for minimum cost operation if reviews are made in accordance with the ERP and a 50 week year is assumed?

Answer. $S = 35 - s$

REFERENCES

1. ARROW, K. J., HARRIS, T. and MARSCHAK, J., 'Optimal Inventory Policy', *Econometrica*, **19**, No. 3, 250 (1951).
2. ARROW, K. J., KARLIN, S. and SCARF, H., *Studies in the Mathematical Theory of Inventory and Production*, Stanford University Press (1958).
3. ALFANDARY-ALEXANDER, M., *An Enquiry into some Models of Inventory Systems*, University of Pittsburgh Press (1962).
4. MAGEE, J. F., *Production Planning and Inventory Control*, McGraw-Hill, New York (1958).
5. LEWIS, C. D., 'An Iterative Analog Inventory Policy Cost Model', *Int. J. Prod. Res.*, **6**, No. 2, 135 (1968).

CHAPTER 6

In-process Inventories: Inventory Queues

The Formation and Description of Queues

Queues, or waiting lines exist in many everyday situations and not all of these are obvious at first sight. Waiting in orderly lines for a bus or for lunch at a self-service counter are evidently queueing situations. Telephone subscribers waiting for an operator to accept a trunk call are equally involved in a queueing situation, but because the other members of the queue are not visible the queueing effect is not so evident.

In a manufacturing situation, work or parts passing from one process to the next can be regarded as queues being *generated* by the earlier processes and requiring *service* from the subsequent processes. Similarly the supply of spare parts can be considered as a queueing situation in which a queue of equipment waits for service in the form of the spare parts being fitted.

Generally then waiting lines occur because the arrivals for a certain service are not dealt with immediately by the server and this 'mismatch' of supply and demand for that service causes a queue to form. Such a queue is completely defined by the arrival pattern of customers requiring the service being offered, the number of servers available to provide that service, the servers' individual service patterns and the queue discipline (i.e. the rules to which queue members conform).

The Arrival Pattern

This can be described most simply by the distribution of the inter-arrival times. It is usually assumed that arrivals occur singly, simultaneous arrivals being treated as zero interarrival times as might happen when customers requiring service arrive collectively in a bus, train, lift, etc.

Where more than one queue exists, the condition of the queues at any instant of time may well influence the individual queue arrival pattern. In a two queue situation, it is evident that a long queue will usually increase the arrival rate of the competing queue—but this may not necessarily be so. Consider the seasoned commuter given the choice of two bus stops, one of which has no queue at all. If the existing queue at the other bus stop is not too long he will most likely join it on the assumption that a bus has recently called at the empty bus stop, and that he stands a better chance of catching an earlier bus at the stop with a queue. However, if the queue is too long he may choose to start one at the empty bus stop on the assumption that even if a bus should come to the other stop first, the length of the queue would make it unlikely for him to get on that bus anyway.

The Service Pattern

The service pattern of each individual server can be described by the distribution of times required for providing the particular service being offered. If delays occur between services this must be taken into account. In the telephone situation, the length of calls represents the service time, for the service being provided is that of equipment availability to connect two particular subscribers.

A more complex service time situation exists, however, at a traffic junction where the service being provided is that of the right to proceed. This is controlled not only by the light colour intervals, but also by the individual car's position in the queue, and the behaviour of the vehicles in front.

The Queue Discipline

This describes the behaviour or rules, to which members of a queue conform. The most common queue discipline perhaps is that of 'first in, first out' (FIFO) which generally prevails in the bus stop and self-service counter type of situation. In most cases where parts are stacked, however, a policy of 'last in, first out' (LIFO) is virtually essential if confusion is to be avoided.

QUEUES OCCURRING IN INDUSTRIAL PROCESSES

The queues so far described are those which occur in everyday life. It is now necessary to describe and identify the types of queue that occur naturally, or that are deliberately introduced in manufacturing situations.

General In-process Stocks

These can be readily identified in most types of production situation and particularly in batch production. Such stocks are usually in the form of bins and pallets of piece parts or sub-assemblies located within the production area. The function of these in-process stocks is essentially that of a temporary store, because as it is expected that such parts will be required in the very near future, it is assumed to be uneconomic to book such material into an officially designated store through the standard procedure. Such stocks provide a decoupling stage between the producing sections generating the queue of in-process stocks and the receiving sections which use these parts in the manufacturing process, and as such service the queue. The existence of the in-process stocks allows both the producing and user sections to work independently of each other within certain limitations.

Buffer Stocks for In-line Transfer Machines

These are stocks of parts held between stages of automatic assembly machines. These stocks provide a similar decoupling function to those mentioned above, but because in this situation all stages of the transfer machine operate simultaneously and usually on a short time cycle, their decoupling effect is much more evident.

For an in-line transfer machine without the provision of buffer stocks, any failure of any stage of the machine causes a total machine failure. With buffer stocks available, however, a single stage failure causes only a partial machine failure for these two reasons:

(a) Early stages are not immediately stopped due to a failure of a later stage, as the earlier stages can continue to produce until the available buffer storage space between the relevant stages is completely filled.

(b) Later stages are not immediately halted by a failure or stoppage of an earlier stage, because these stages can continue until all the supplying buffer stock is exhausted.

Machine Interference

This name is given to the situation where one or a limited number of operatives are employed to service several machines. The queue is represented by the machines waiting either for service in the form of more material, a machine fault clearance or repair. The idle machines obviously represent a loss of production and an underutilisation of plant, and the problem posed is essentially one of minimising the number of idle machines with a minimum number of operatives, taking into account the relative cost of both. For readers interested in this topic, the monograph by Cox and Smith[1] is recommended.

Spare Parts and Replacement

In this problem the situation is similar to the last one, but here the supply of spare parts is the major factor influencing the repair of equipment, rather than whether labour is available to fit such parts. The basic question posed is to estimate how many spare parts should be held available in stock for a failure of that part in service, knowing that costs are involved both in holding spares and also in not replacing failed parts immediately. Also in the machine interference situation, the supply of material for restarting is usually more important than either fault clearance or repair. In this spare part situation, however, the supply of material in that particular sense does not enter into the problem.

The formulation of spare part inventory policies will be considered more fully in Chapter 7, and has already been examined to some extent in Chapter 4 in which one of the joint calculation of re-order levels and replenishment order quantities models considered a spare part type of situation.

THE CLASSICAL APPROACH TO THE SINGLE-SERVER QUEUE WITH RANDOM ARRIVALS AND EXPONENTIAL SERVICE-TIMES

In a queueing situation in which a single server deals with a stream of customers arriving randomly at an average rate λ and the distribution of arrivals is Poisson, then the probability that exactly n arrivals occur in a time interval t is given by:

$$P(n) = \frac{(\lambda t)^n e^{-\lambda t}}{n!} \tag{6.1}$$

where λt is obviously the mean number of arrivals in that interval t. Fig. 6.1 shows graphical plots for $P(n)$ as a function of n for several values of λt.

The Poisson distribution has been found to represent approximately many arrival distributions in practice, some examples being the

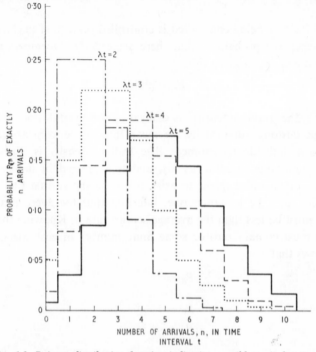

Fig. 6.1. *Poisson distribution function indicating possible arrival patterns*

births per day in a hospital and, as has been noted earlier, the pattern of demand at a retail level. Evidence of the likelihood of a Poisson distribution is also often associated with queueing situations where the probability of an event occurring is independent of previous events.

If members of the queue are served at a mean rate μ, and the distribution of resulting service times is assumed to be exponential, then the probability that a queue member having entered service at time zero, has completed that service between time t and $(t+dt)$ is μdt and is independent of the time so far spent in service. Thus the probability that, having entered service at time zero, a queue member is still receiving service at time t is given by:

$$P(\geq t) = e^{-\mu t}$$

If the queue being considered is controlled on a 'first in, first out' basis, then the probability that there are exactly n members in the whole queue, P_n, is given by:

$$P_n = \varrho^n P_0 \qquad (6.2)$$

where ϱ the 'traffic intensity' is defined as the mean service time of a single customer divided by the mean interval between arrivals of successive individual customers. The traffic intensity is, therefore, evaluated in this situation as λ/μ and is expressed in units called erlangs. For a stable queue to exist, it can be shown that the traffic intensity must be less than one, inferring that the average arrival rate λ must be less than the average service rate μ. Knowing that the queue must contain zero or some finite number of customers, then it follows that

$$\sum_{n=0}^{\infty} P_n = 1$$

and thus
$$P_0 = 1 - \varrho$$
and
$$P_n = \varrho^n(1-\varrho) \qquad (6.3)$$

from which it is evident that ϱ can also be described as the proportion of time the server is occupied.

To find $\bar{n}$ the average number of all queue members either waiting or being served; it is necessary to sum from zero to infinity the product of n and the probability that there are exactly n queue members, thus:

$$\bar{n} = \sum_{n=0}^{\infty} nP_n = \sum_{n=0}^{\infty} n\varrho^n P_0$$

$$\bar{n} = \frac{\varrho}{1-\varrho} \qquad (6.4)$$

and the mean queue length $\bar{q}$ of the $(n-1)$ queue members still waiting for service is given by:

$$\bar{q} = \sum_{n=1}^{\infty} (n-1)P_n = \sum_{n=1}^{\infty} (n-1)\varrho^n P_0$$

$$\therefore \quad \bar{q} = \frac{\varrho^2}{1-\varrho} \tag{6.5}$$

and as the average time spent both waiting in the queue and being served, $\bar{t}$, is given by $\bar{n}$ (the average number of queue members either waiting or being serviced) multiplied by $1/\mu$ (the mean service time) then:

$$\bar{t} = \frac{\bar{n}}{\mu} = \frac{1}{\mu} \cdot \frac{\varrho}{1-\varrho} \tag{6.6}$$

and this indicates the delay to queue members caused by the queue.

Table 6.1 indicates values of the average whole queue length $\bar{n}$ and the average queue length $\bar{q}$ for different values of ϱ the traffic intensity. It should be noted how rapidly congestion, as represented by queue length, builds up as traffic intensity approaches unity.

Fig. 6.2 shows the average delay in minutes caused by a queue for differing values of both ϱ the traffic intensity and μ the average hourly service rate.

Table 6.1. VALUES OF WHOLE QUEUE AND QUEUE LENGTH FOR A SIMPLE QUEUEING SITUATION

Traffic intensity ϱ	Average whole queue length $\bar{n} = \varrho/(1-\varrho)$	Average queue length $\bar{q} = \varrho^2/(1-\varrho)$
0·1	0·111	0·011
0·2	0·250	0·050
0·3	0·429	0·129
0·4	0·667	0·267
0·5	1·000	0·500
0·6	1·500	0·900
0·7	2·333	1·633
0·8	4·000	3·200
0·9	9·000	8·100

A more comprehensive set of graphs of delays caused by queueing can be found in Buchan and Koenigsberg.[2]

The queueing model described here, of Poisson arrivals and exponential service, is one of the simplest types mathematically and has been presented briefly to indicate the general approach made to such

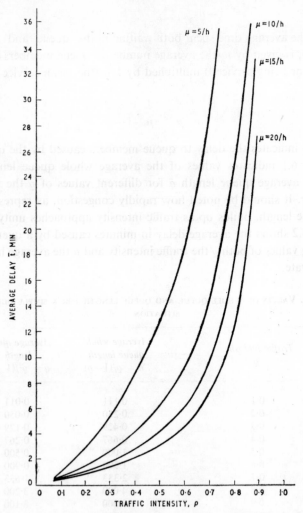

Fig. 6.2. Delays caused at differing traffic intensities and hourly service rates

problems. Many more complicated queueing situations have been considered in various excellent texts on queueing theory[1, 3, 4] some of which are listed below.

(a) The single server queue with random arrivals with either fixed service times or generally distributed service times.
(b) Single server queue with arrival rates and service rates dependent on queue size.
(c) Queues with multiple servers.
(d) Multiple queues in parallel and series combinations.

For the more complex queueing situations like those described by (d) the mathematical description of the model becomes very complicated. So much so that for many practical queueing situations which do occur, complete mathematical analysis has so far proved impossible. It is mainly for this reason that simulation has been resorted to in this field in an attempt to analyse practical queueing problems. It is largely because these simulation models themselves become very cumbersome if written in traditional computer languages of the Fortran type, that higher order languages such as SIMSCRIPT and C.S.L. have been developed.

BUFFER STOCKS FOR IN-LINE TRANSFER MACHINES

Considering a two stage element of an in-line transfer machine, in which both stages can fail either simultaneously or independently of each other, it is evident that there are four possible conditions that can occur at each machining cycle. These are:

(a) Both stages can operate. Here there is no change in the level of the buffer stock held between the two stages.
(b) Both stages can fail. Again there is no change in the buffer stock level.
(c) The first stage can operate and the second stage fail. Assuming that buffer storage space is available, this situation increases the buffer stocks held by one unit.

(*d*) The first stage can fail but the second stage can operate if any buffer stock is available. The buffer stock is then depleted by one unit.

This buffer storage situation can be considered as a discrete level, single server queue with random arrivals in discrete time and random services in discrete time. The first stage acts as a generator of parts forming the queue of buffer stock requiring service from the second stage, and the fluctuations of the size of this queue due to the four

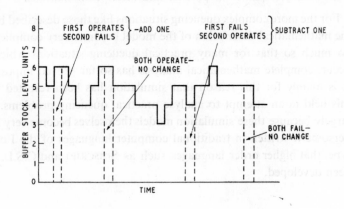

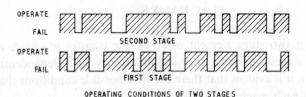

Fig. 6.3. *Buffer stocks held between two stages of an in-line transfer machine*

possible combinations of circumstance already detailed can be clearly seen in Fig. 6.3. The behaviour of this type of queue is known as that of a 'birth-death' process in discrete time such that the state of the queue at any time $(t+1)$ can be expressed in terms of the queue state at time t and the failure probabilities of the first stage (ϕ_1) and the second stage (ϕ_2) such that:

$$P_n(t+1) = P_n(t)[(1-\phi_1)(1-\phi_2)+\phi_1\phi_2]$$
$$+P_{n+1}(t)[\phi_1(1-\phi_2)]+P_{n-1}(t)[\phi_1(1-\phi_2)]$$

where $P_n(t)$ is the probability of there being just n units of buffer stock at time t.

From this consideration it can be shown that the traffic intensity for this situation assuming infinite buffer storage is given by:

$$\varrho = \frac{\phi_2(1-\phi_1)}{\phi_1(1-\phi_2)} \qquad (6.7)$$

from which it is evident that the probability of there being no buffer stock $P_o(t)$ is given by:

$$P_o(t) = 1-\varrho = \frac{\phi_1-\phi_2}{\phi_1(1-\phi_2)} \qquad (6.8)$$

The above results can be used further to explain some interesting aspects of this particular type of queue's behaviour. Some of these will now be investigated with the aim of providing the reader with a better understanding of the function of queues generally.

For the condition where the amount of buffer storage is assumed not to be limited, for a stable queue to exist $\varrho < 1$,

$$\therefore \qquad \frac{\phi_2(1-\phi_1)}{\phi_1(1-\phi_2)} < 1$$

from which it can be seen that $\phi_2 < \phi_1$.

This indicates, as one would expect, that for the size of the buffer stock to be described by a stable queue the first stage of the in-line transfer machine must fail more frequently than the second.

Investigating the twin reasons for holding buffer stock, it can be said that:

For the second stage to be able to operate in spite of a failure of the first stage, it should not have failed and some buffer stock should exist. The probability of this happening, $P_{\bar{1}2}(t)$, can be evaluated as:

$$P_{\bar{1}2}(t) = \varrho(1-\phi_2)\phi_1$$
$$= \phi_2(1-\phi_1)$$

For the first stage to be allowed to continue to operate (even though the second stage fails) because buffer storage space is available, the first stage should not fail and the second stage should fail. Therefore, the probability of this happening, $P_{1\bar{2}}(t)$, is given by:

$$P_{1\bar{2}}(t) = \phi_2(1-\phi_1)$$

Thus it can be seen that the advantage gained by incorporating a buffer stock system in an in-line transfer machine is divided equally between allowing the first stage to continue operating when the second has failed, and thus adding one unit to the buffer stock; also allowing the second stage to continue operating when a failure occurs at the first stage but buffer stock is available and is thereby depleted by one unit.

The output of such a two-stage system with buffer storage can be found by considering the proportion of time that both stages operate simultaneously or that the second stage operates, the first fails and at least one unit of buffer stock is available. This proportion of time that output is generated from the second stage P_{out} can then be evaluated as;

$$P_{out} = (1-\phi_1)(1-\phi_2)+\phi_2(1-\phi_1)$$
$$\therefore \quad P_{out} = 1-\phi_1 \tag{6.9}$$

This indicates that the output of the two stages combined is completely dependent on the probability of the first stage working, which must be true since for a stable queue this first stage must fail more frequently than the second, and work passing through the first stage must eventually be processed by the second.

The increase in the proportion of time that the in-line transfer machine produces output as a result of allowing buffer storage is given by P_{out} minus the joint probability that both stages operate simultaneously, i.e. $(1-\phi_1)(1-\phi_2)$, and this can be shown to equal $\phi_2(1-\phi_1)$.

Table 6.2 indicates various parameters of such an interstage buffer storage situation for differing values of failure probabilities of both stages.

Table 6.2. INTER-STAGE BUFFER STORE PARAMETERS

Probability of 1st stage failing ϕ_1	Probability of 2nd stage failing ϕ_2	Traffic intensity $\dfrac{\phi_2(1-\phi_1)}{\phi_1(1-\phi_2)}$	Proportion of time output is generated without buffer storage $(1-\phi_1)(1-\phi_2)$	Proportion of time output is generated with buffer storage $(1-\phi_1)$	Increase due to buffer storage $\phi_2(1-\phi_1)$
0·9	0·8	0·445	0·02	0·10	0·08
	0·7	0·260	0·03	0·10	0·07
	0·6	0·167	0·04	0·10	0·06
	0·5	0·115	0·05	0·10	0·05
	0·4	0·074	0·06	0·10	0·04
	0·3	0·048	0·07	0·10	0·03
	0·2	0·028	0·08	0·10	0·02
	0·1	0·012	0·09	0·10	0·01
0·8	0·7	0·667	0·06	0·20	0·14
	0·6	0·375	0·08	0·20	0·12
	0·5	0·250	0·10	0·20	0·10
	0·4	0·167	0·12	0·20	0·08
	0·3	0·107	0·14	0·20	0·06
	0·2	0·062	0·16	0·20	0·04
	0·1	0·028	0·18	0·20	0·02
0·7	0·6	0·642	0·12	0·30	0·18
	0·5	0·429	0·15	0·30	0·15
	0·4	0·285	0·18	0·30	0·12
	0·3	0·184	0·21	0·30	0·09
	0·2	0·107	0·24	0·30	0·06
	0·1	0·048	0·27	0·30	0·03
0·6	0·5	0·667	0·20	0·40	0·20
	0·4	0·445	0·24	0·40	0·16
	0·3	0·285	0·28	0·40	0·12
	0·2	0·167	0·32	0·40	0·08
	0·1	0·074	0·36	0·40	0·04
0·5	0·4	0·667	0·30	0·50	0·20
	0·3	0·429	0·35	0·50	0·15
	0·2	0·250	0·40	0·50	0·10
	0·1	0·115	0·45	0·50	0·05
0·4	0·3	0·642	0·42	0·60	0·18
	0·2	0·375	0·48	0·60	0·12
	0·1	0·167	0·54	0·60	0·06
0·3	0·2	0·585	0·56	0·70	0·14
	0·1	0·260	0·63	0·70	0·07
0·2	0·1	0·445	0·72	0·80	0·08

This two-stage buffer storage problem with synchronous operations at both stages is obviously one of the simplest buffer storage situations that could be considered analytically but it does present several characteristics which are still evident in more complex situations. One is that for a stable queue to exist earlier stages must fail more frequently than subsequent stages. Also the function of such a buffer store is divided equally between allowing earlier stages to continue operation when later stages have failed, and allowing later stages to continue operation when earlier stages have failed but units of buffer storage exist. Of these dual functions, it is only the latter which contributes directly to increased output.

Other buffer storage situations which have been considered analytically are:

(*a*) Multiple stages with infinite queues allowed in front of all stages.

(*b*) Multiple unsynchronised stages with no queues allowed between stages with the exception of the first which is allowed an infinite queue. Vacant stages are allowed but the restriction imposed for transfer of work between stages is that work can only leave one stage when the subsequent stage is free or vacant.

(*c*) Multiple stages with finite queues allowed between stages but with an infinite queue permitted in front of the first stage.

(*d*) No interstage queues allowed with the exception of the first, and no vacant stages allowed, i.e. no stage can pass on work until all stages have completed their individual operations.

It is evident, from the discussion in this chapter, that the topic of queueing and buffer storage is one aspect of inventory control in which theory lags practice. None of the models noted here comes anywhere near the complexity of many existing production units functioning most efficiently in industry to-day. However, even though the theory of queues may not be able to determine exactly the behaviour patterns of these more complex practical situations, the conclusions drawn concerning the characteristics of simple queues can be used as indicators of what is likely to happen.

As has been mentioned earlier, the use of recently developed computer languages specifically for simulation, has provided a new technique in approaching the analysis of such problems.

EXERCISES

1. If customers arriving randomly at a queue are dealt with on average once every two minutes but are delayed on average by five minutes, what must their average arrival rate be if service times are assumed to be exponential?

Answer. One every three minutes approximately

2. For the above situation what is the percentage probability that one customer is in service and one waiting in the queue?

Answer. 14·6 per cent

3. For a two-stage in-line transfer machine situation, show that the percentage increase in output derived as a result of allowing buffer storage depends entirely on ϕ_2, the probability of failure of the second stage. Assume that theoretically infinite storage is allowed between the two stages but that the queue representing buffer stock is basically stable

Answer Percentage increase as a result of allowing storage, $100\phi_2/(1-\phi_2)$.

4. For an in-line transfer machine for which the permitting of buffer stock increases output by 25 per cent, what is the probability of failure of the first stage if the queue representing the buffer stock operates at a traffic intensity of 0·6 erlangs?

Answer. $\phi_1 = 0{\cdot}295$ as $\phi_2 = 0{\cdot}2$

REFERENCES

1. Cox, D. R. and Smith, W. L., *Queues*, Methuen Monograph on Applied Probability and Statistics, Methuen, London (1961).
2. Buchan, J. and Koenigsberg, E., *Scientific Inventory Management*, Prentice-Hall Inc., Englewood Cliffs (1963).
3. Cruon, R. (Ed.), *Queueing Theory–Recent Developments and Applications*, English Universities Press, London (1967).
4. Morse, P. M., *Queues, Inventories and Maintenance*, Wiley, New York (1958).

Queueing Tables

Peck, L. G. and Hazelwood, R. N., *Finite Queueing Tables*, Wiley, New York (1958).

CHAPTER 7

Inventory Queue of Slow-moving Spare Parts

Most of the inventory situations considered so far have assumed adequate records of past demand data for use in predicting future trends, and have by inference assumed that the average stock held to meet this demand was certainly non-zero. In the slow-moving spare parts situation, however, where demand for an item occurs only very occasionally, past records rarely if ever extend far enough back in time to determine future trends with any reasonable degree of statistical confidence. Also the stockholding decisions presented by this type of situation more usually consider the choice of whether to hold one unit of stock or none at all, rather than in the traditional inventory problem as to what average level stock should be held to meet demand economically. It is apparent therefore that when demand per unit time for an item is typically zero, one or two, that a different approach to the stockholding policy must be made.

Mitchell[1] in his article and review details the National Coal Board's approach to this problem, and produces a very simple chart method (which is generally applicable) for determining whether to hold zero, one, two or three spare parts depending on the particular spare part's ratio of stockout cost to purchase cost, the incidence of failure and the leadtime involved in obtaining a new spare part.

Mitchell indicates that the importance of slow-moving spares (usually engineering spares) mainly due to their relatively high cost has been noted by such organisations as the R.A.F., the U.S.A.F., the U.S. Navy and the French steel industry. These organisations have found that a large proportion of their money invested in stocks was tied up in a relatively few expensive spare parts. It was also noted that for all engineering spares the proportion with low consumption probably increased with the value of the item considered and this suggested a high concentration of stock value in expensive slow-moving spare parts.

Apart from the problem of the likely inadequacy of past records of slow-moving spare parts, an associated problem is that of the shortness of the effective life of the plant for which the spare part is ostensibly being held. If the effective life is only of the order of four or five years, which is often the case now-a-days with improvements in plant design, etc., it could well be that the plant could complete this period without ever requiring a particular spare part. Even where the plant has been in use sufficiently long for consumption patterns to be established, because of the length of time involved, records of spare part usage may often be inadequately documented and a failure to record one usage in this type of situation will usually invalidate any conclusions drawn. Another problem of examining records taken over such a long period is that the plant could well be running under different operating conditions during the period, with different usage requirements of spares associated with each separate operating condition.

Some of the problems noted above can be somewhat overcome if several identical pieces of plant are operated under identical conditions. Here the aggregate usage is more likely to be determined with a reasonable statistical confidence. However, although an organisation may operate several identical pieces of plant, these are usually situated at different locations and therefore by inference are operating under different conditions. Even should the situation exist where several pieces of identical plant were being operated under identical conditions, the aggregate usage for spares is no longer one of slow-moving spares in the true sense, as it can be regarded as a relatively fast-moving stock item, even though made up of slow-moving items. Some thoughts have been given to the improved aggregation of spare part usage throughout an organisation by the introduction of standardisation of plant, but this is obviously very much a long-term remedy, as renewal of plant simply to improve the prediction of the usage of spares will hardly, if ever, be economically justifiable.

A further difficulty with slow-moving spares is their inflexibility. Whereas the overstocking of fast-moving spares is quickly remedied by natural consumption, this is not the case with slow-moving spares. Initially such over-buying can be remedied only slowly, particularly if the spare is unique to one particular piece of plant, thus making it impossible to transfer it elsewhere or to sell it to other manufacturing organisations. For unique spares, when the plant for which such parts are being held closes or becomes obsolete any spares left over are worth only their scrap value.

Initial over-buying is not the only cause of excess stocking of slow-moving spares. Fast-moving stock items can easily be adjusted to allow for short-term variations in leadtimes. But for slow-moving stocks an increase in stocks to compensate for a short-term lengthening of leadtimes may lead to serious over-stocking when leadtimes return to normal.

Any policy for slow-moving spares must take into account the stockout costs involved when, as a result of not having a spare part available, plant lies idle. To estimate accurately this cost of stockout can present further difficulties, but fortunately due to the limited number of decisions which are available in operating a policy for slow-moving spares, costs incurred due to inaccuracies in estimating the value of the stockout costs are not large, and do not often alter the *correct* decision to one that is less correct. Very rarely does one need to hold more than one or two spare parts of the slow-moving variety, and thus the number of possible decisions is limited to just three, namely, whether to hold zero, one or two.

CLASSIFICATION OF SLOW-MOVING SPARES

Mitchell indicates that not all spares are held as insurance or stand-by spares in the normal sense of being held to cut the cost of a breakdown. Any method of control devised for general use must therefore take into account the different types of slow-moving spare for which it is to be used. The classification selected must be as simple as is consistent with proper control. The classification given below has been agreed as a result of discussions between engineers and operational research scientists in the coal industry and has been accepted as reasonable and practicable. It is in no way peculiar to the coal industry.

Specials

These are items which have been bought for use on a certain date, for example in preparation for a major overhaul of certain plant. Provided the manufacturer is given sufficient warning of the requirement and keeps to the date agreed, and provided he is informed of any change of plan delaying the item's use, there is no reason why specials should be held in stock longer than the time taken to examine them prior to use. Stocks of such items can therefore be controlled very closely.

Adequate Warning Items

These either have a minor breakdown but can be economically patched up for a period longer than the leadtime, or their wear indicates, by a period longer than the leadtime, the impending breakdown. Spares for these items should not be held in stock, but frequently are.

True Stand-by Spares

These give either no warning or inadequate warning of breakdown.
The engineers do not intend to use them on a particular data, but
hold them because they consider it cheaper to do so than stand the
extra cost of a breakdown due to their not being available. These spares
can be classified one stage further according to the life characteristics
of the parent part. Some parts break down randomly and the optimum
stockholding policy does not vary. Others wear out and have a failure
rate which increases with their life. These are known as 'wear' items.
Economies can be effected in the stocking of such items by deferring
the purchase of the replacement spare after one is used.

Fig. 7.1 shows the above classification diagrammatically together
with the recommended methods of control.

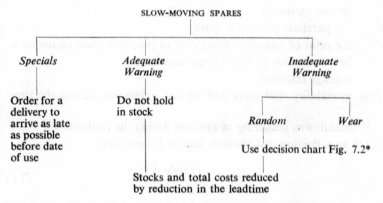

Fig. 7.1. Classification of slow-moving spares and the recommended method of control

SUMMARY OF RECOMMENDED METHODS
OF CONTROL

Specials. These should be ordered so that delivery occurs as shortly
as possible prior to use.

* The derivation of this decision chart follows immediately.

Adequate Warning Items. These should be ordered when the warning occurs unless the patch-up time is known to be significantly longer than the leadtime.

Stand–by Spares. Use decision chart, Fig. 7.2.

DERIVATION OF CONTROL PROCEDURES

Random Breakdown Spares

For the analysis of random breakdown spares the following notation is adopted:

τ average time between demands

C_o average ordering cost

C_s stockout cost (the average extra cost each time a demand cannot be met ex-stock)

C_p the purchase price of a spare

i the ratio of annual holding cost to purchase price (assumed to be 10 per cent in this spares situation)

$\bar{L}$ average leadtime

$P(n)$ probability that there will be just n demands during the time.

If breakdowns occurring at random during the leadtime are distributed as a Poisson distribution, then it follows that:

$$P(n) = \frac{(\bar{L}/r)^n e^{-\bar{L}/r}}{n!} \tag{7.1}$$

For a re-order level system with unit order quantity and non-captive* demand, Karush[2] has indicated the steady state probability solution of this system. From Karush's analysis it follows that the

---

* Captive demand means that in a stockout, the demand is met by early delivery of one of the spares on order. Non-captive demand means that a stockout is met from some other source. Making the required part in the workshop or having it transferred from a neighbouring branch would imply non-captive demand.

average annual cost in the steady state with maximum stock N is:

$$C_N = iC_p \left[N - \frac{L}{\tau} \left\{ \sum_{n=0}^{N-1} P(n) \middle/ \sum_{n=0}^{N} P(n) \right\} \right]$$

$$+ \frac{C_s}{\tau} \left\{ P(N) \middle/ \sum_{n=0}^{N} P(n) \right\} + \frac{C_o}{\tau} \left\{ 1 - P(N) \middle/ \sum_{n=0}^{N} P(n) \right\} \quad (7.2)$$

From Eqn. (7.2), obviously one requires to find that value of N which minimises C_N, and Mitchell develops a very simple graphical method of doing this, using Fig. 7.2. Here the curves $C_0 = C_1$ (i.e. the points at which an equal cost is involved in stocking either zero or one spare part) and $C_1 = C_2$ (i.e. the points at which equal costs are involved in holding either one or two spare parts) are plotted on a graph of C_s/C_p, the ratio of the stockout cost to the purchase price, against τ the average time between demands. The curve $C_0 = C_1$ is independent of the average leadtime required to replace a spare part, but the curve $C_1 = C_2$ is not, and is therefore drawn for various values of average leadtime from one month to two years.

The use of this chart simplifies considerably the decision of whether to hold zero, one or two spare parts compared with the rather complex expression of Eqn. (7.2). For those spare parts whose value of C_s/C_p and τ correspond to a point lying below the curve $C_0 = C_1$, no spares should be held; for those lying above $C_0 = C_1$ and below the relevant curve $C_1 = C_2$, one should be held; and for those lying above $C_1 = C_2$ two spares should be held. For any points lying exactly on $C_1 = C_2$ or $C_0 = C_1$, there is obviously no difference in the costs involved in deciding to hold two or one, or one or zero spare parts respectively. The curves of $C_2 = C_3$ have not been drawn, as the decision to hold up to three spares is not considered.

Fig. 7.2 is drawn up on the assumption that the annual cost of holding a spare is equal to 10 per cent of its price, demand is non-captive and that the time to obsolescence is greater than 15 years. It can be shown that whether demand is either captive or non-captive does not have much influence on the decision of how many spares should be stocked to minimise annual operating costs.

9

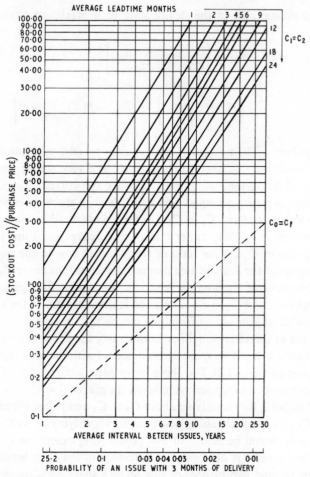

Fig. 7.2. Chart for deciding stock policy for stand-by spares

Wear Items

The identification of true wear items when only a few failures have occurred is indeed difficult and can often be inferred only intuitively from the original definition of a wear item, namely, that such a part's failure rate increases with its length of life. However, if items can be identified as true wear items, Mitchell shows using reliability functions,[3] that if the probability of usage of the spare three months after delivery subject to its not being required earlier can be estimated from past data, then the decision of whether to place an order for just one spare part or to defer an order for one spare part can again be made using Fig. 7.2. In this wear situation, if the point specified by the stockout cost and the purchase price of the spare part and the probability of its being used within three months of delivery (as read from the additional horizontal scale and assuming now a fixed leadtime) lies below the line $C_1 = C_0$ the order is deferred. If however the point so specified lies above $C_1 = C_0$ an order for one spare part is placed immediately.

Further analysis by Mitchell shows that costs of operating a slow-moving spare part inventory system can be brought down considerably by reducing the effective leadtime required to replace a part when the decision has been made to order. The only part of the leadtime which is under the direct control of the organisation requiring the spare part is the time involved in informing the manufacturer of the spare that it is required. Thus, whenever a decision is made to order a further spare part, using any of the forgoing methods, this should be organised to be fed through as quickly as possible to the purchasing department actually placing the order. It may also be beneficial in cost to try to influence the supplier of the slow-moving spare part by offering additional financial rewards for shorter delivery times in an attempt to reduce the overall leadtime.

EXERCISES

1. If the stockout cost of an item is known to be £300 and its purchase price £10, would it be economic to hold two of this item in stock if the leadtime involved in obtaining a replacement part from an outside manufacturer is a year and the part fails randomly (on average) once every five years?

Answer. No, slightly more economic to hold one

2. If for an item costing £30 it is known to be equally economic to hold in stock either none or one, what is the assumed stockout cost associated with that item if it fails randomly (on average) once every four years?

Answer. £12

3. If it were discovered that the item described in Question 2 was a true 'wear' item, with a probability of usage of 3 per cent within three months of receipt, would it be economic to defer the placing of a replacement order until a further review?

Answer. Yes

REFERENCES

1. MITCHELL, G. H., 'Problems of Controlling Slow-Moving Spares', *Opl Res. Q.*, **13**, No. 1, 23 (1962).
2. KARUSH, W., 'A Queueing Model for an Inventory Problem', *Opl Res. Q.*, **5**, No. 5 (1957).
3. A.R.I.N.C. RESEARCH CORPORATION, *Reliability Engineering*, Prentice Hall, New Jersey (1965).

CHAPTER 8

Multi-product Inventory Situations

Very few inventory systems in practice are concerned with controlling just a single item of stock. In spite of this, all the inventory models considered so far have been concerned exclusively with such single-product situations. This approach has thus ignored the possible inter-action effects that could arise when more than one product is being considered. To remedy this the present chapter will discuss exclusively what happens in the multi-product situation when certain limiting restrictions exist on such things as invested capital, storage space or machining facilities.

In the single-product situation, the imposition of a restriction impo-ses no real problem analytically as the parameters of the inventory control system can be adjusted easily to meet that particular restriction without being concerned with the imputed ones arising from the inter-action effects caused by other products. For instance, a restriction on capital imposed on a single item being controlled by a re-order level policy, if it is required to maintain the same level of customer protec-tion, can be met only by a reduction in the replenishment order quan-tity. This particular action causes replenishment orders to be placed more frequently thus producing an increased cost of ordering and an overall increase in inventory operating costs. When the same capital restriction is applied to a mixture of stocked items however, replenishment orders again have to be reduced in size to meet the restriction (again at an increased operating cost) but now the proportion by which each individual replenishment order size should be reduced is no longer directly apparent.

CALCULATION OF THE MODIFIED ECONOMIC ORDER SIZES WHEN A LIMITATION IS SET ON CAPITAL INVESTED IN STOCKS

Where management decide to limit the amount of capital invested in stocked items, should the average capital invested in stocks of all items when using the unrestricted replenishment order sizes (such as the economic order quantity) exceed the capital restriction, obviously the calculation of the replenishment order quantities must be modified.

If a capital restriction is not in effect, then V, the average total value invested in stocks, would be given by:

$$V = g \sum_{j=1}^{J} q_j C_{m_j} \qquad (8.1)$$

where q_j is the replenishment order quantity for the jth item

C_{m_j} is the per unit material and labour cost or work's prime cost of the jth item

g is the so called 'normalising factor'

This normalising factor g is introduced to allow for replenishment orders for individual items arriving at different times rather than simultaneously. Should it so happen that all replenishment orders were received simultaneously, it would produce a maximum investment situation and the value of g would therefore be one. If, however, it is assumed that the receipt of replenishment orders is spread over time such that capital investment is half the maximum value, then g would equal one-half. Generally it can be assumed that g lies somewhere between a value of one-half and one, the exact figure depending on the particular situation.

Assuming that V the average total value invested in stocks exceeds $V_{\max}$ (the average maximum value allowed by management), the problem is to know in what manner each individual item's replenishment order size should be reduced to meet effectively this overall capital restriction.

Thus we have the condition

$$V_{max} \geqslant V = g \sum_{j=1}^{J} q_j C_{m_j}$$

or, alternatively,

$$V_{max} - g \sum_{j=1}^{J} q_j C_{m_j} \geqslant 0 \qquad (8.2)$$

An indeterminate Lagrange multiplier z can then be defined by:

$$z < 0 \quad \text{when} \quad V_{max} - g \sum_{j=1}^{J} q_j C_{m_j} = 0$$

$$z = 0 \quad \text{when} \quad V_{max} - g \sum_{j=1}^{K} q_j C_{m_j} < 0$$

As $z \left\{ V_{max} - g \sum_{j=1}^{J} q_j C_{m_j} \right\}$ is always zero by definition, the total annual inventory operating cost (excluding stockout costs and letting the holding cost for the jth item be represented by $C_{m_j}i$) can then be given by:

$$C = \sum_{j=1}^{J} \left\{ \frac{C_{o_j} A_j}{q_j} + \frac{q_j C_{m_j} i}{2} \right\} + z \left\{ V_{max} - g \sum_{j=1}^{J} q_j C_{m_j} \right\} \qquad (8.3)$$

To minimise this total operating cost function, C is differentiated with respect to q_j and the result set equal to zero thus:

$$\frac{dC}{dq_j} = -\frac{C_{o_j} A_j}{q_j^2} = \frac{C_{m_j} i}{2} - zg C_{m_j} = 0$$

Re-writing q_j now as Q'_{o_j}, the modified economic order quantity we obtain:

$$Q'_{o_j} = \sqrt{\frac{2 C_{o_j} A_j}{C_{m_j}(i - 2gz)}} \qquad (8.4)$$

At this stage it is generally recommended (see Buchan and Koenigsberg,[1] p. 318 or Thompson[2] p. 125) that different increasing values of z

should be tried until the capital restriction is just met. This procedure can become very tedious especially if no computer is easily accessible, and it should be avoided if at all possible. For this particular model of a multi-product inventory system subject to a single restriction on capital, because the material cost C_{m_j} is a common factor to both the cost of holding inventory and the capital invested, it is possible to evaluate z directly as follows:

Q'_{o_j} the modified economic order quantity can be rewritten in terms of the unrestricted economic order quantity as:

$$Q'_{o_j} = Q_{o_j} \sqrt{\frac{i}{i - 2gz}} \tag{8.5}$$

Now ideally we wish that

$$V_{\max} - g \sum_{j=1}^{J} Q'_{o_j} C_{m_j} = 0$$

and substituting for Q'_{o_j} using Eqn. (8.5) this then becomes

$$V_{\max} - g \sqrt{\frac{i}{i - 2gz}} \sum_{j=1}^{J} Q_{o_j} C_{m_j} = 0 \tag{8.6}$$

Thus if the maximum possible capital invested, $g \sum_{j=1}^{J} Q_{o_j} C_{m_j}$, is calculated and the average maximum capital allowed, $V_{\max}$, is known, z can be evaluated directly using

$$z = -\frac{i}{2g} \left[\left(\frac{g \sum_{j=1}^{J} Q_{o_j} C_{m_j}}{V_{\max}} \right)^2 - 1 \right] \tag{8.7}$$

In practice, however, to calculate the modified replenishment order quantities required to meet the capital restriction, it is not necessary to actually calculate z as these order sizes can be evaluated from the unrestricted economic order quantity Q_{o_j} and the value of $\sqrt{\{i/(i - 2gz)\}}$ which from Eqn. (8.5) is given by:

$$\sqrt{\frac{i}{i - 2gz}} = \frac{V_{\max}}{g \sum_{j=1}^{J} Q_{o_j} C_{m_j}} \tag{8.8}$$

Now it is apparent from the very concept of economic order quantity theory, that because the replenishment order sizes have been reduced to accommodate the capital investment restriction, the total inventory operating costs must increase as a result of the restriction being in force compared with the unrestricted case. This rise in operating costs results because the increased cost of ordering smaller replenishment orders more frequently is not offset by the reduced holding costs accrued from lower average inventory levels.

It follows that the total inventory operating costs C for the unrestricted situation is given by:

$$C = \sum_{j=1}^{J} \left\{ \frac{C_{o_j} A_j}{Q_{o_j}} + \frac{Q_{o_j} C_{m_j} i}{2} \right\}$$

and this expression can be very much simplified by substitution and then becomes:

$$C = i \sum_{j=1}^{J} Q_{o_j} C_{m_j} \tag{8.9}$$

C' the annual inventory operating cost for the restricted situation is given by:

$$C' = \sum_{j=1}^{J} \left\{ \frac{C_{o_j} A_j}{Q'_{o_j}} + \frac{Q_{o_j} C_{m_j} i}{2} \right\}$$

which also by substitution can be shown to be:

$$C' = (i - gz) \sqrt{\frac{i}{i - 2gz}} \sum_{j=1}^{J} Q_{o_j} C_{m_j}$$

or more simply as:

$$C' = \frac{1}{g} \{(i - gz) V_{\max}\} \tag{8.10}$$

SIGNIFICANCE OF THE LAGRANGE MULTIPLIER z

Defining δC as the increased annual operating cost due to the imposition of the capital restriction, this can be evaluated as $C' - C$ which when substituting from Eqns. (8.9) and (8.10) can be defined as:

$$\delta C = \left[(i - gz) \sqrt{\frac{i}{i - 2gz}} - i \right] \sum_{j=1}^{J} Q_{o_j} C_{m_j}$$

If for most practical situations it can be assumed that $\sqrt{\{i/(i-2gz)\}}$ is approximately unity, then:

$$\delta C \doteqdot -z \left\{ g \sum_{j=1}^{J} Q_{o_j} C_{m_j} \right\}$$

Thus, z can be considered as the unit proportional increase in annual inventory operating costs resulting from the imposition of the capital restriction.

LEVEL AT WHICH THE INCREASED INVENTORY OPERATING COSTS BECOME PROHIBITIVE

It would be useful to know at what value of the Lagrange multiplier z the increase in inventory operating costs resulting from the capital restriction becomes prohibitive. In Chapter 3 it was indicated generally that below a value of $Q_{45°}$ (the minimum economic order quantity which subtends an angle of $45°$ with the horizontal) the gradient of the cost versus order quantity curve increased at such a rate as to make operation below this point uneconomic.

Now if we require that no modified economic order quantity should fall below its $Q_{45°}$ value as a result of the capital restriction, if follows that:

$$Q'_{o_j} \geqslant Q_{45°_j}$$

Thus

$$\sqrt{\frac{2C_{o_j}A_j}{C_{m_j}(i-2gz)}} \geqslant \sqrt{\frac{2C_{o_j}A_j}{iC_m+2}}$$

which can be simplified down to

$$-z \leqslant \frac{1}{gC_{m_j}}$$

For the first individual item whose modified economic order quantity (which as a result of increasing z in an attempt to meet the capital restriction) falls below its particular value of $Q_{45°}$, it follows that:

$$-z \leqslant \frac{1}{C_{m_{max}}} \tag{8.11}$$

where $C_{m_{max}}$ is the highest material and labour or works prime cost for any individual item in the group.

Substituting for this value of z in Eqn. (8.6), V_{min}, the minimum capital investment level below which it would not be advisable to operate because of the increased annual inventory operating costs, is given by:

$$V_{min} \geqslant \sqrt{\frac{iC_{m_{max}}}{iC_{m_{max}}+2}} \, g \sum_{j=1}^{J} Q_{o_j} C_{m_j} \tag{8.12}$$

Thus, if the solution of a multi-product capital restriction problem is solved for a value of z greater than $1/gC_{m_{max}}$, or if the capital restriction is below V_{min}, it can be assumed that the capital restriction is unrealistic in-so-far that it causes an excessive increase in inventory operating costs. Above the value of V_{min}, small variations in the value of z do not cause significant alterations in the inventory operating costs.

Example (Invested Capital Restriction)

For the data provided, what replenishment order sizes should be used for each of the four inventory items considered if the limit on invested capital is £130 when operating with an assumed normalising factor of 0·5 and a holding interest rate of 20 per cent? At what annual inventory operating cost is this capital restriction achieved and at what capital restriction level would these operating costs become prohibitive?

Inventory item	Annual usage A_j	Unit material and labour cost or works prime cost C_{m_j}, p	Ordering or set-up cost C_{o_j}, p	Unrestricted economic order quantity Q_{o_j}
1	10 000	25	50	447
2	6 000	20	50	387
3	3 000	40	50	194
4	2 000	15	50	258

Checking initially to make sure that the capital invested in stocks when using the unrestricted economic order quantities does exceed the £130 restriction, we require to evaluate:

$$g \sum_{j=1}^{4} Q_{o_j} C_{m_j} = 0·5[447(1/4)+387(1/5)+194(2/5)+258(3/20)]$$

$$= £152·72 \text{ which certainly exceeds the £130 restriction}$$

To discover by what factor the unrestricted economic order quantities should be multiplied to meet the capital restriction we require to evaluate $\sqrt{\{i/(i-2gz)\}}$ which from Eqn. (8.8) can be calculated for this particular problem as $130/152·72 = 0·85$.

Thus
$$Q'_{o_1} = 447 \times 0·85 = 377 \text{ units}$$
$$Q'_{o_2} = 387 \times 0·85 = 330 \text{ units}$$
$$Q'_{o_3} = 194 \times 0·85 = 165 \text{ units}$$
and
$$Q'_{o_4} = 285 \times 0·85 = 219 \text{ units}$$

Checking to see that these replenishment order sizes do in fact bring the average capital invested to £130 approximately we evaluate:

$$g \sum_{j=1}^{4} Q'_{o_j} C_{m_j} = 0·5[377(1/4)+330(1/5)+165(2/5)+219(3/20)]$$

$$= £129·50$$

This meeting of the capital restriction is achieved by using a value of z which is given by:

$$z = -0.2\left[\left(\frac{152.72}{130}\right)^2 - 1\right] = -0.078$$

Now $\quad C = i\sum_{j=1}^{J} Q_{o_j}C_{m_j} = 0.2\times305.44 = £61.09$

and $\quad C' = \frac{(i-gz)}{g}V_{max} = \frac{(0.2+0.5\times0.078)\times130}{0.5} = £62.14$

Therefore δC, the increase in inventory operating costs caused by the capital restriction, $= C'-C = £(62.14-61.09) = £1.05$ and as a rough check:

$$\delta C \doteq -z\left[g\sum_{j=1}^{J}Q_{o_j}C_{m_j}\right] = 0.078(152.72) = £1.19$$

For the increased inventory operating costs to become prohibitive due to the capital restriction it follows that:

$$V_{min} \geqslant \sqrt{\frac{iC_{m_{max}}}{2+iCg}\sum_{j=1}^{4}Q_{o_j}C_{m_j}}$$

$$\geqslant \sqrt{\frac{0.2\times8}{2+0.2\times8}}\times152.72$$

$$V_{min} \geqslant £102$$

Therefore, below an invested capital limit of £102, the increase in inventory operating costs would make the whole inventory operation uneconomic.

Fig. 8.1 shows the print-out of the solution to the same problem solved iteratively on a computer, and the encircled entry in the $g = 0.5$ column confirms the value of z as being about -0.08, the inventory operating costs at that point being £62.

NORMALISING FACTOR G	0.46	0.48	0.50	0.52	0.54
	CAPITAL		INVESTED £		
$Z = -0.070$	122.2	126.8	131.4	136.0	140.5
$Z = -0.075$	*****	*****	130.2	134.7	139.2
$Z = -0.080$	*****	*****	129.1	133.5	137.8
$Z = -0.085$	*****	*****	*****	132.3	136.6
$Z = -0.090$	*****	*****	*****	131.1	135.3
$Z = -0.095$	*****	*****	*****	129.9	134.1
$Z = -0.100$	*****	*****	*****	*****	132.9
$Z = -0.105$	*****	*****	*****	*****	131.8
$Z = -0.110$	*****	*****	*****	*****	130.6
$Z = -0.115$	*****	*****	*****	*****	129.6
RESTRICTED OPERATING COST (£)	61.7	61.7	62.0	62.3	62.9

REPLENISHMENT ORDERS REQUIRED TO MEET CAPITAL LIMITATION

	0.46	0.48	0.50	0.52	0.54
ITEM 1	389.0	386.9	378.0	365.9	351.3
ITEM 2	336.8	335.1	327.3	316.9	304.2
ITEM 3	168.4	167.5	163.7	158.4	152.1
ITEM 4	224.6	223.4	218.2	211.2	202.8

UNRESTRICTED OPERATING COST = £ 61.09
EOQS

ITEM 1 = 447.2
ITEM 2 = 387.3
ITEM 3 = 193.6
ITEM 4 = 258.2

CAPITAL LIMITATION PROBLEM

Fig. 8.1. Computer print-out for capital limitation problem

CALCULATION OF THE MODIFIED ECONOMIC ORDER SIZES WHEN A LIMITATION IS SET ON TOTAL STORAGE SPACE

Where the maximum allowable total* storage space is limited to a value S_{max}, the average value of the space occupied by stocks would be given by S as:

$$S = g \sum_{j=1}^{J} q_j W_j \qquad (8.13)$$

where W_j is the storage space required per unit for the jth item
g is again a normalising factor with a similar range of values to that considered earlier for the capital restriction case

Following through the same stages as for the capital restriction model we have:

$$S_{max} - g \sum_{j=1}^{J} q_j W_j \geqslant 0 \qquad (8.14)$$

and the same procedure would eventually produce the value of the modified economic order quantity Q''_{o_j} under this storage space restriction as:

$$Q''_{o_j} = \sqrt{\frac{2C_{o_j}A_j}{iC_{m_j} - 2\theta g W_j}} \qquad (8.15)$$

where θ is again an indeterminate Lagrange multiplier.

For this particular multi-product model where a limitation is placed on storage space, no further simplification is possible and successive values of the modified economic order quantities must, therefore, be evaluated for different increasing values of θ until the total space limitation expressed by the restriction equation of (8.13) is just met.

The value for the Lagrange multiplier can be considered as the imputed rental value per cubic foot of storage space. Thus if the value of θ found to solve this space restriction model is greater than the

---

*(indicating that there is no specific space limitation for individual items within the multi-product group).

NORMALISING FACTOR G	0.46	0.48	0.50	0.52	0.54
			STORAGE	SPACE	
$\theta = -0.070$	1180.	1227.	1273.	1319.	1365.
$\theta = -0.085$	*****	1204.	1249.	1293.	1337.
$\theta = -0.100$	*****	1183.	1226.	1269.	1312.
$\theta = -0.115$	*****	*****	1205.	1247.	1288.
$\theta = -0.130$	*****	*****	1185.	1226.	1266.
$\theta = -0.145$	*****	*****	*****	1206.	1245.
$\theta = -0.160$	*****	*****	*****	1187.	1225.
$\theta = -0.175$	*****	*****	*****	*****	1207.
$\theta = -0.190$	*****	*****	*****	*****	1189.
$\theta = -0.205$	*****	*****	*****	*****	*****
RESTRICTED OPERATING COST (£)	61.3	61.5	61.8	62.1	62.5

REPLENISHMENT ORDERS REQUIRED TO MEET STORAGE LIMITATION

ITEM 1	433.5	427.2	420.7	414.1	407.4
ITEM 2	359.4	347.8	336.5	325.5	314.9
ITEM 3	182.9	178.3	173.6	169.1	164.6
ITEM 4	216.0	201.6	189.0	177.8	167.8

UNRESTRICTED OPERATING COST = £ 61.09
EOQS

ITEM 1 = 447.2
ITEM 2 = 387.3
ITEM 3 = 193.6
ITEM 4 = 258.2

STORAGE SPACE LIMITATION PROBLEM

Fig. 8.2. Computer print-out for storage space limitation problem

known rental value of storage space, additional storage space should be rented to reduce the overall inventory operating costs.

The iterative calculation procedure required to solve the storage space limitation problem is best performed on a computer. A print-out of a computer solution to the problem indicated below is shown in Fig. 8.2. The data for this problem is the same as that considered previously for the capital restriction case but in addition the storage space for each individual item is indicated and a total storage space restriction exercised.

Example (Storage Space Restriction)

For the data provided below, what replenishment order sizes should be used for each item if the limit on storage space is $1\,200$ ft³, and at what percentage increase in inventory operating costs does this occur?

Inventory item	Annual usage A_j	Unit material and labour cost or work's prime cost C_{m_j}, p	Ordering or set-up cost C_{0_j}, p	Storage space per item W_j, ft³	Unrestricted economic order quantity Q_{0_j}
1	10 000	25	50	1	447
2	6 000	20	50	2	387
3	3 000	40	50	3	194
4	2 000	15	50	4	258

Total average space required for storage is given by:

$$S = g \sum_{j=1}^{J} Q_{0_j} W_j = 0\cdot5[447(1) + 387(2) + 194(3) + 258(4)]$$

$$= 1\,417\cdot5 \text{ ft}^3$$

This certainly exceeds the limit placed on storage space of $1\,200$ ft³ and, therefore, all economic order quantities must be reduced to

10

meet this restriction. The computer print-out indicates that this restriction is just met (with $g = 0.5$ and $i = 20$ per cent) at the position indicated by $\theta = -0.130$ for which the modified economic order quantities are to the nearest whole number 421, 337, 174 and 189 for items 1, 2, 3 and 4 respectively. These quantities produce an annual inventory operating cost of £61·8 which is a 1·2 per cent increase on the unrestricted case of £61·09.

CALCULATION OF THE MODIFIED ECONOMIC ORDER SIZES WHEN A LIMITATION IS SET ON THE ANNUAL AGGREGATE SET-UP TIME

A very common restriction present in many manufacturing concerns is that of machine availability. Other than by installing additional equipment, the only ways that one can ensure improved machine utilisation are either to improve loading schedules or restrict severely the time for which machines are allowed to lie idle during set-ups. This latter can be achieved by limiting the number of fresh production runs (each involving a set-up period) and thus reducing the overall time due to set-ups.

If T is defined as the annual aggregate time limit placed on the set-up times for a group of items, this restriction can be expressed as:

$$T - \sum_{j=1}^{J} \frac{A_j t_j}{q_j} \geqslant 0 \qquad (8.16)$$

where A_j/q_j is the number of set-ups for the jth item per annum

t_j is the set-up time required for a production run of any length q for the jth item

Before proceeding, it is interesting to note that this restriction is non-linear, as the time limit is proportional to the reciprocal of the order size q. In the two previous situations considered of capital and storage space limitations however, the restrictions were linear, being directly proportional to the order size q. These features can be illustrated by considering a two-product situation (which is conveniently represented pictorially in two dimensions) with either a capital/storage space limitation or an aggregate set-up time limitation. These two situations are shown as Figs. 8.3(a) and 8.3(b) respectively.

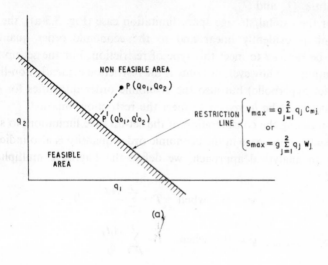

NON FEASIBLE AREA

$P(Q_{o_1}, Q_{o_2})$

$P'(Q'_{o_1}, Q'_{o_2})$

q_2

FEASIBLE AREA

q_1

RESTRICTION LINE $\begin{cases} V_{max} = g \sum\limits_{j=1}^{2} q_j\, c_{mj} \\ \text{or} \\ S_{max} = g \sum\limits_{j=1}^{2} q_j\, W_j \end{cases}$

(a)

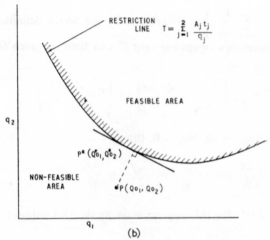

RESTRICTION LINE $\quad T = \sum\limits_{j=1}^{2} \dfrac{A_j\, t_j}{q_j}$

FEASIBLE AREA

q_2

$P^*(\hat{Q}_{o_1}, \hat{Q}_{o_2})$

NON-FEASIBLE AREA

$P(Q_{o_1}, Q_{o_2})$

q_1

(b)

Fig. 8.3. Two-product system under
(a) linear restriction   (b) non-linear restriction

In both these diagrams, the point P represents the operating position when the true economic order quantities Q_{o_1} and Q_{o_2} are used. Point P' represents the minimum cost solution when the relevant restriction is imposed and is, therefore, defined by the modified economic order quantities Q'_{o_1} and Q'_{o_2}.

For the capital/storage space limitation case (Fig. 8.3(a)), the restriction is evidently linear and to the economic order quantitity must be *reduced* to meet this type of restriction. For the set-up time limitation case however, not only is the restriction evidently non-linear (in fact hyperbolic) but also the economic order quantities for each product must be *increased* to meet the restriction imposed.

Continuing the consideration of the set-up time limitation, to show that such an increase in the economic order quantity is also indicated from an analytical approach, we define the Lagrange multiplier ψ thus:

$$\psi < 0 \quad \text{when} \quad T - \sum_{j=1}^{J} \frac{A_j t_j}{q_j} = 0$$

$$\psi = 0 \quad \text{when} \quad T - \sum_{j=1}^{J} \frac{A_j t_j}{q_j} > 0$$

Now as $\psi \left\{ T - \sum_{j=1}^{'} \frac{A_j t_j}{q_j} \right\}$ is always zero by the above definition, the total annual inventory operating cost C can then be given for this situation by:

$$C = \sum_{j=1}^{J} \left\{ \frac{C_{oj} A_j}{q_j} + \frac{q_j C_{mj} i}{2} \right\} + \psi \left\{ T - \sum_{j=1}^{J} \frac{A_j t_j}{q_j} \right\} \qquad (8.17)$$

To minimise C we set $\mathrm{d}C/\mathrm{d}q_j = 0$, thus:

$$\frac{\mathrm{d}C}{\mathrm{d}q_j} = -\frac{C_{oj} A_j}{q_j^2} + \frac{C_{mj} i}{2} + \psi \frac{A_j t_j}{q_j^2} = 0$$

Rewriting q_j as $Q_{o_j}^*$, for this aggregate set-up time limitation case, we obtain:

$$Q_{o_j}^* = \sqrt{\left\{ \frac{2A_j(C_{oj} - \psi t_j)}{i C_{mj}} \right\}} \qquad (8.18)$$

As ψ by definition is always negative, whenever the limitation on aggregate set-up time is violated then $Q_{o_j}^* > Q_{o_j}$, indicating that order quantities must always be increased above the values of the economic order quantities if the restriction is to be met.

As with the two other restriction models considered, the implementation of this set-up limitation here is achieved only at the expense of increasing the inventory operating costs. Here the cost increase results from the increase in inventory holding costs due to the larger batch sizes not being offset by the reduction in ordering costs accrued from the placing of fewer orders for production runs.

Again, for this set-up time limitation model, these is no easy way of finding the required value of ψ and an iterative calculation procedure must be resorted to. This is illustrated by another example using the same data as previously but now indicating item set-up times and limiting the aggregate annual set-up time.

Example (Aggregate Set-Up Time Restriction)

It can be shown for the situation described by the data below, that for a five day, 50 week year, setting up represents 25 per cent of the possible machining time available when operating with manufacturing runs based on economic order quantities. Management are no longer prepared to accept this situation and have placed a restriction of 20 per cent on set-up times. What production run lengths must be used to meet this restriction and what is the percentage increase in operating costs resulting from operating with these values?

Inventory item	Annual usage A_j	Unit material and labour cost or work's prime cost C_{m_j}, p	Ordering or set-up cost C_{o_j}, p	Set-up time t_j, days	Unrestricted economic order quantity Q_{o_j}
1	10 000	25	50	$\frac{1}{2}$	447
2	6 000	20	50	1	387
3	3 000	40	50	$1\frac{1}{2}$	194
4	2 000	15	50	2	258

AGGREGATE

SET-UP TIME

(DAYS)

$\psi = -$	0.00	65.51
$\psi = -$	2.00	58.23
$\psi = -$	4.00	53.42
$\psi = -$	6.00	49.35
$\psi = -$	8.00	*****
$\psi = -$	10.00	*****
$\psi = -$	12.00	*****
$\psi = -$	14.00	*****

RESTRICTED OPERATING COST = £ 62.79

REPLENISHMENT ORDERS REQUIRED TO
MEET SET-UP TIME LIMITATION

ITEM 1	510.0
ITEM 2	490.1
ITEM 3	266.8
ITEM 4	382.5

UNRESTRICTED OPERATING COST = £ 61.09

EOQS

ITEM 1 =	447.2
ITEM 2 =	387.3
ITEM 3 =	266.8
ITEM 4 =	382.5

AGGREGATE SEP-UP TIME LIMITATION PROBLEM

Fig. 8.4. Computer print-out for set-up time limitation problem

The unrestricted aggregate annual set-up times is given by:

$$\sum_{j=1}^{4} \frac{A_j t_j}{Q_{o_j}} = \left[\frac{10\,000}{477} \left(\frac{1}{2}\right) + \frac{6\,000}{387} (1) + \frac{3\,000}{194} \left(1\frac{1}{2}\right) + \frac{2\,000}{258} (2) \right]$$

$$= 65{\cdot}5 \text{ days}$$

For a five day week, 50 week year this represents $\frac{65{\cdot}5}{250} \times 100 = 25$ per cent of the possible machining time. If this is restricted now to 20 per cent it means that $T = 0{\cdot}2 \times 250 = 50$ days set-up per year.

The results of a computer solution to this problem are again shown as a print-out in Fig. 8.4 and indicate that the order quantities or run lengths required to meet this restriction are 510, 490, 267 and 383 for items 1, 2, 3 and 4 respectively. This is achieved by operating at an annual inventory operating cost of £62·79, which is a 2·8 per cent increase over £61·09 cost of using the unrestricted economic order quantities.

CALCULATION OF THE MODIFIED ECONOMIC ORDER QUANTITY WHEN A LIMITATION IS SET ON BOTH INVESTED CAPITAL AND ANNUAL AGGREGATE SET-UP TIME

The three models dealt with so far in this chapter have been concerned only with single restrictions. Now we shall deal with a problem involving the dual restrictions of invested capital and aggregate annual set-up time. Such a problem requires both a linear and non-linear restriction to be met simultaneously and it is quite possible that there will be no satisfactory solution to the problem. It will be remembered that the limitation on invested capital requires smaller replenishment order sizes than the economic order quantity, but that the aggregate annual set-up time limitation required production runs longer than the economic order quantity. Thus it is apparent that unless a solution to these conflicting requirements is found somewhere near the value of the economic order quantity, it is highly unlikely that any solution will be found at all.

Referring, as an example of this, to the two product problem illustrated in Figs. 8.5(a) and 8.5(b), where the restrictions are as shown in Fig. 8.5(a), there is no possible solution since the two individual feasible areas of solution do not overlap; where the restric-

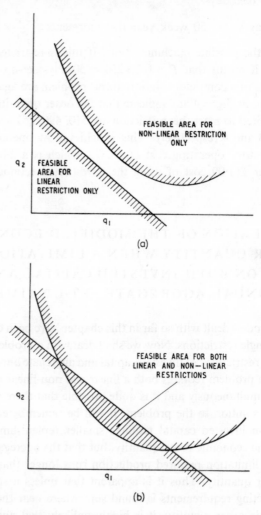

Fig. 8.5. *Two-product system under dual restrictions for which there is (a) no feasible solution (b) an area of feasible solutions*

tions are as shown in Fig. 8.5(b), however, because the two feasible areas do overlap, a series of solutions (one of which will minimise the inventory operating costs) can be found.

For the multi-product system subject to a limitation on invested capital and a further limitation on aggregate annual set-up time, it follows from previous considerations that the annual inventory operating cost can be expressed as:

$$C = \sum_{j=1}^{J} \left\{ \frac{C_{oj}A_j}{q_j} + \frac{q_j C_{mj} i}{2} \right\} + z \left\{ V_{\max} - g \sum_{j=1}^{J} q_j C_{mj} \right\}$$

$$+ \psi \left\{ T - \sum_{j=1}^{J} \frac{A_j t_j}{q_j} \right\} \tag{8.19}$$

from which for a minimum

$$\frac{dC}{dq_j} = \frac{C_{oj}A_j}{q_j^2} + \frac{C_{mj} i}{2} - zg C_{mj} + \psi \frac{A_j t_j}{q_j^2}$$

From this it can be shown that the order quantity which could satisfy both restrictions and at the same time minimise inventory operating costs is given by:

$$q_j = \sqrt{\left\{ \frac{2A_j(C_{oj} - \psi t_j)}{C_m(i - 2zg)} \right\}} \tag{8.20}$$

The solution to this dual restriction problem can only be found by using an iterative computation procedure in which both z and ψ are varied simultaneously in an attempt to find a feasible solution.

CALCULATION OF THE MODIFIED ECONOMIC ORDER QUANTITY WHEN A LIMITATION IS SET ON STORAGE SPACE AND AGGREGATE ANNUAL SET-UP TIME

Using a similar approach to that just made and replacing the invested capital restriction by a limitation on storage space, it can be shown that the order size which could satisfy both the aggregate set-up time limitation and the limitation on storage space at minimum cost is given by:

$$q_j = \sqrt{\left\{ \frac{2A_j(C_{o_j} - \psi t_j)}{C_{m_j}i - 2\theta g W_j} \right\}} \tag{8.21}$$

CONCLUSION

This chapter has indicated the manner in which replenishment order sizes should be modified, by either increasing or decreasing their values below that of the economic order quantity, in order to meet some specified restriction or restrictions. The imposition of any restriction is bound to increase inventory operating costs compared with the economic order quantity situation, but these increases are not excessive unless unrealistic restrictions are imposed. A major drawback with most of the methods of solution, however, is that an iterative calculation procedure is required and this can become very tedious when considering even a few products. For this reason calculations are best carried out on a computer if this is possible.

EXERCISES

To avoid iterative calculations only the capital restriction model will be considered in these examples ($i = 20\%$).

Item	Annual usage A_j	Material or works prime cost C_{m_j}, p	Ordering cost C_{o_j}, p	Economic order quantity Q_{o_j}
1	5 000	30	60	315
2	3 000	20	60	300
3	4 000	15	60	400

For the three products listed above, if a restriction of £100 were imposed on invested capital what should be the relevant order size for each item assuming a normalising factor of 50 per cent? What is the value of the Lagrange multiplier in this situation?

Answer. 295, 280 and 373 units respectively, $z = -0.03512$

2. What is the inventory operating cost both with and without the restriction, and at what value would the restriction become too costly to operate?

Answer. £21·75 and £21·45 respectively. At a value of £66

REFERENCES

1. BUCHAN, J. and KOENIGSBERG, E., *Scientific Inventory Management*, Prentice-Hall (1963).
2. THOMPSON, W. W., *Operations Research Techniques*, C. E. Merrill Books Inc. (1967).

CHAPTER 9

Coverage Analysis

'Coverage analysis' is the name given to an inventory control technique developed by J. Murdoch* and others. Murdoch has defined the main objective of coverage analysis as being the minimisation of capital invested in inventory throughout the whole range of stocked items, subject to keeping the total number of replenishment orders placed per annum constant at the same figure existing before the introduction of the scheme.

It is proposed that this concept can eliminate many of the difficulties experienced in operating an inventory control system based on economic order quantity formulae.

Further objectives put forward for the technique are that:

(a) The technique must provide a quantitative estimate of the reduction in stock capital brought about as a result of its application

(b) The technique should be based on statistical sampling theory to enable analysis to be carried out quickly and efficiently

The coverage G of an item is defined as the ratio of the average stock level of an item to its annual usage, thus:

* Senior Lecturer, College of Aeronautics, Cranfield.

$$G = \frac{\text{average stock level}}{\text{Annual usage}}$$

$$G = \frac{I}{A}$$

For a re-order cycle type of policy, and also for a re-order level policy if R is made zero, the average stock level for any item can be shown to be given by:

$$I = \frac{q}{2} + k\sigma_d \sqrt{(R+\bar{L})} \tag{9.1}$$

thus the coverage G of an item is given by:

$$G = \frac{I}{A} = \frac{1}{2m} + \frac{k\sigma_d \sqrt{(R+\bar{L})}}{A} \tag{9.2}$$

where m is the number of orders placed per year and is equivalent to A/q.

By plotting graphically the coverage versus the number of replenishment orders placed per annum as in Fig. 9.1, it can be seen that

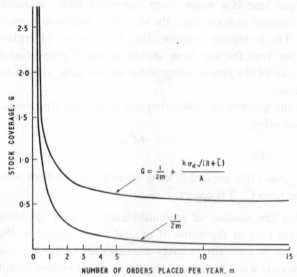

Fig. 9.1. Relationship between number of orders placed per annum and coverage

for any reasonable number of replenishments per year the value of the coverage becomes independent of such replenishments because $1/2m$ decreases rapidly above a figure of $m = 10$. The diagram also indicates clearly that the relative importance of the two components of coverage varies with changes in the number of replenishments per year. When this number is low, a greater proportion of coverage is attributed to active stock but as the replenishments per year increase a higher proportion of the coverage is attributable to the safety stock.

Thus it is possible to describe the characteristics of a particular inventory item in terms of its coverage value as follows:

$G = \infty$, represents dead stock

G over 2, slow moving stock

G less than one, normal turnover stock

$G = 0$, no stock

Coverage analysis claims that the number of replenishments orders placed per year is a much more important factor in reducing the capital invested in stocks than the size of the individual replenishment orders. The technique proposes that the number of replenishment orders per year for any item should be made proportional to the square root of the annual usage value of that item, subject to certain restrictions.

Thus the number of replenishments m_j for the jth item would be evaluated using:

$$m_j \propto A_j C_{m_j}$$

given that either

(a) C_{o_j} and i (the implied holding interest rate) are both constant, or
(b) the ratio C_{o_j}/i is constant.

Making the number of replenishments per year proportional to the square root of the value of annual usage subject to the above restrictions, is generally suitably applied only to bought out items, and then only when the changes in the resulting replenishment orders sizes are not substantial.

In practice it is obviously impossible to estimate the constant of proportionality required to calculate m_j for each individual item such that $\sum_{j=1}^{N} m_j$ remains the same as before coverage analysis was introduced; therefore a system of grouping is adopted. For a sample size of N of between 200 to 500 stocked items it is usual, when applying coverage analysis, to split the items by annual usage value into between eight and twelve classes. Ideally, to simplify calculation, the class intervals should be chosen such that the square root of each class mid-point value is a real number. Two suitable examples of such a grouping procedure are shown in Tables 9.1(a) and 9.1(b). Obviously the units of the class intervals can be in either pounds or shillings whichever is suitable. It is possible to evaluate other class groupings, but readers will find it easier to use either part of this table, but multiplied by a suitable proportioning factor to obtain a table appropriate to their needs. The square root of the mid-point value should be multiplied directly by the proportioning factor and the class interval, and mid-point values by the square of the factor used.

Table 9.1a. CLASS GROUPING BY VALUE OF ANNUAL USAGE FOR A RANGE 0–30 000

Class	Class interval	Mid-point	Mid-point	Theoretical number of replenishments per item per annum in this class, *Y*
1	0– 50	25	5	1
2	51– 150	100	10	2
3	151– 650	400	20	4
4	651– 1 150	900	30	6
5	1 151– 1 950	1 600	40	8
6	1 951– 3 050	2 500	50	10
7	3 051– 4 150	3 600	60	12
8	4 151– 8 650	6 400	80	16
9	8 651–30 000	19 600	140	28

Table 9.1b. CLASS GROUPING BY VALUE USAGE FOR A RANGE 0–360

Class	Class interval	Mid-point	Mid-point	Theoretical number of replenishments per item per annum in this class, Y
1	0– 2	1	1	1
2	3– 5	4	2	2
3	6– 12	9	3	3
4	13– 19	16	4	4
5	20– 30	25	5	5
6	31– 41	36	6	6
7	42– 86	64	8	8
8	87–113	100	10	10
9	114–174	144	12	12
10	175–217	296	14	14
11	218–360	289	17	17

PROCEDURE FOR CALCULATING NUMBER OF REPLENISHMENTS WHEN THESE ARE PROPORTIONAL TO THE SQUARE ROOT OF THE VALUE OF ANNUAL USAGE

Table 9.2 is used in calculating the proposed number of replenishments per item when these should be proportional to the square root of the value of annual usage. The procedure is best considered step-by-step:

(a) Divide the inventory items into their various class categories based on value of annual usage, preferably using one of the standard class interval tables which will then provide real numbers as mid-point values.

(b) Record how many items fall into each class (column E).

(c) Record the total number of replenishments per annum placed at present for the items falling into each of these classes (column F).

Table 9.2. LAYOUT FOR CALCULATING THE REPLENISHMENTS PER YEAR FOR COVERAGE ANALYSIS SYSTEM WHERE THESE ARE PRO-PORTIONAL TO THE SQUARE ROOT OF THE ANNUAL USAGE VALUE OF THE CLASS

| A | B | C | D $= \sqrt{C}$ | E | Present policy | | Proposed policy | | |
| | | | | | F | G $= F/E$ | H $= (D/5)Y$ | I $= E \times H$ | J $= H(Y)$ |
Class	Value of annual usage A_jC_{mj}	Mid-point C_{mj}	Square root of mid-point	Num-ber of items in this class	Total number of replenish-ments/annum	Average number of replenishments/item/annum (rounded off)	Theoretical number of replenish-ments/item/annum, Y	Theoretical total number of replenish-ments/annum, Y	Actual number of replenish-ments/item/annum (rounded off)
1	0– 50	25	5	5	13	3	1	5	1
2	51– 150	100	10	13	70	5	2	26	2
3	151– 300	225	15	34	143	5	3	102	3
4	301– 500	400	20	37	183	5	4	148	4
5	501– 1 300	900	30	76	517	7	6	456	5
6	1 301– 3 700	2 500	50	46	390	8	10	460	9
7	3 701– 6 100	4 900	70	11	113	10	14	154	12
8	6 101–10 100	8 100	90	8	85	10	18	144	16
9	10 101–14 100	12 100	110	5	34	7	22	110	19
10	14 101–19 700	16 900	130	6	54	9	26	156	23
11	19 701–25 300	2 250	150	4	57	14	30	120	26
				245	1 659			1 881Y	

1 881Y = 1 659   thus   Y = 0·88

(d) Calculate the average number of replenishments placed per annum, rounding off to the nearest whole number (column $G = F/E$).

(e) For each class calculate the theoretical total number of replenishments by multiplying the number of items in the class by the corresponding theoretical number of replenishments per item per annum (column $I = E \times H$).

(f) Sum the theoretical number of total replenishments over all classes (i.e. sum column I which in this case comes to $1\,881Y$).

(g) Equate the theoretical number of total replenishments over all classes with the actual number of replenishments placed over all classes at present. (This is the sum of column $F = 1\,659$ which therefore is equated with $1\,881Y$.)

(h) Calculate the proportioning factor Y (equal to 0·88).

(i) By substituting for Y in the theoretical number of replenishments per item per annum, and rounding off to the nearest whole number, the actual number of proposed replenishments per item per annum in each class can finally be evaluated (column $J = H(Y)$).

Looking now in some detail at the results of applying such a procedure to the information given in Table 9.2, it is interesting to note the differences in the proposed and present number of replenishments per item per annum; for ease of presentation these are extracted and presented separately as Table 9.3.

From Table 9.3 it can be seen that for items in the low value of annual usage classes (i.e. classes 1–5) it is proposed to place fewer replenishment orders per annum than at present, thus increasing the

Table 9.3. COMPARISON OF PRESENT AND PROPOSED REPLENISHMENTS PER ANNUM PER ITEM

Class	1	2	3	4	5	6	7	8	9	10	11
Average present replenishments/annum/ item	3	5	4	5	7	8	10	10	7	9	14
Proposed replenishments/annum/item	1	2	3	4	5	9	12	16	19	23	26

capital invested in stocks in this range. However, for those items falling into high value annual usage classes (i.e. classes 6–11) it is proposed that more replenishment orders are placed per annum, thus reducing the capital invested in stocks at this end of the range. The aim of this method of calculating the number of replenishments per year however is to achieve an overall reduction in capital invested when considering all classes.

CALCULATION OF THE REPLENISHMENT ORDER QUANTITY REQUIRED FOR THE PROPOSED NEW ORDERING SYSTEM

The method described for calculating the number of replenishments per year was based on the concept that for each item the number of replenishments per annum was made proportional to the value of annual usage, thus:

$$m_j = Z \sqrt{A_j C_{m_j}} \tag{9.3}$$

where Z is a constant of proportionality which in the example shown in Table 9.3 has a value of 0·2.

Now assuming in the proposed scheme that the annual usage for an individual item remains the same as previously, then:

$$A_j = m_j q_j = Z \sqrt{A_j C_{m_j}} q_j$$

where q_j is the size of the replenishment order for the proposed scheme which can now be evaluated as:

$$q_j = \frac{1}{Z} \sqrt{\frac{A_j}{C_{m_j}}} \tag{9.4}$$

Thus for the example considered here, the size of replenishment orders for individual items which will maintain the same annual usage at the new proposed number of replenishments per item per year will be given by:

$$q_j = 5 \sqrt{\frac{A_j}{C_{m_j}}}$$

11*

PLOTTING THE COVERAGE CURVE

The plotting of the coverage curve (necessary for estimating the reduction in overall capital invested in stocks) could obviously become a very complicated business if great accuracy were required. Fortunately experience in the application of the coverage analysis technique has shown that the plotting of the curve does not need to be very accurate, and simple curve fitting is mostly satisfactory. Fitting by regression analysis need only be resorted to when a reasonable spread of points is not obtained when plotting the individual coverage values for all the inventory items in the sample being considered.

The technique for drawing the coverage curve is first to draw the $1/2m$ hyperbola and to then add the points representing the individual inventory items' coverage values. Knowing that the actual coverage curve must be parallel to the $1/2m$ hyperbola, it is usually a simple matter to draw an approximate coverage curve. For the situation being considered here (the $1/2m$ hyperbola), the inventory item coverage values and the actual coverage curve drawn as a result are shown in Fig. 9.2.

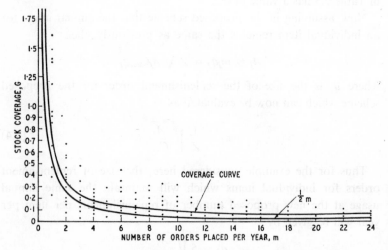

Fig. 9.2. *Inventory item coverage and resultant coverage curve*

CALCULATING THE REDUCTION IN STOCK CAPITAL BROUGHT ABOUT BY THE INTRODUCTION OF COVERAGE ANALYSIS

By definition, estimates of stock capital for both the existing and proposed schemes of replenishment can be calculated for each class of annual usage value as:

Estimate of stock capital = coverage × value of annual usage × number of stock items in the class

Coverage. This can be read from the coverage curve at the value corresponding to the number of replenishments per item per annum figure calculated.

Value of annual usage. This is taken as the mid-point of the class interval.

Number of stock items in the class. This is already known.

By summing the estimates of stock capital over all classes it can then be seen by how much the method of coverage analysis has reduced the capital invested in stock compared with the method of inventory control previously existing.

The relevant data required for this series of calculations has been extracted from Table 9.2 and together with the calculations of the estimates of stock capital are presented in Table 9.4.

From this table it can be seen that the estimates of stock capital using the present method of inventory control remain below those for the proposed system up to the fifth class, thereafter the proposed method produces the lower estimates. Summing overall, the present method produces an estimate of stock capital of 61 108 whereas the proposed method requires only an estimated 46 384. This shows that the application of coverage analysis has reduced the capital invested in stock by some 25 per cent which is of the general order of reduction claimed by supporters of the technique.

Another point worth noting from Table 9.4 is that with the proposed method, coverage declines consistently with increasing annual usage values, whereas for the present method, although coverage does also decline with increasing annual usage values generally, the decline is not always consistent.

Table 9.4. LAYOUT FOR CALCULATING THE PRESENT AND PROPOSED OVERALL ESTIMATES OF STOCK CAPITAL

A Class	B Mid-point of annual usage value, class intervals	C Items in this class	D Present average replenishments/item/annum	E Proposed replenishments/item/annum	F Present coverage	G Proposed coverage	H = B×C×F Estimate of present stock capital	I = B×C×G Estimate of proposed stock capital
1	25	5	3	1	0·24	0·70	30	80
2	100	13	5	2	0·16	0·34	208	545
3	225	34	4	3	0·19	0·24	1 460	1 840
4	400	37	5	4	0·16	0·19	2 380	2 820
5	900	76	7	6	0·12	0·16	8 200	10 900
6	2 500	46	8	10	0·11	0·106	12 700	12 200
7	4 900	11	10	14	0·10	0·086	5 390	4 640
8	8 100	8	10	18	0·10	0·058	6 480	3 758
9	12 100	5	7	22	0·12	0·050	7 260	3 025
10	16 900	6	9	26	0·10	0·040	10 140	4 056
11	22 500	4	14	30	0·076	0·028	6 860	2 520
							61 108	46 384

CONCLUSIONS

The great attraction of coverage analysis as an inventory control technique is that it is specifically devised to cope with a whole range of items rather than with individual items of stock. It achieves this by using several approximating techniques such as statistical sampling, assuming that mean values can represent a whole class of items and can still retain this representation when multiplied by other factors, rounding off and using very rough graph plotting techniques. These approximation techniques will obviously introduce some degree of error, but as with all inventory techniques, is there any point in being too accurate when the data on which calculations are based are themselves not known with any great degree of precision?

Readers of Chapter 8 will realise that a reduction on capital invested in stocks is only one of many criteria on which an inventory control system could be based, although most would perhaps agree that it is one of the most important. Several applications of coverage analysis have shown up to 30 per cent reductions in invested capital, and very few applications are recorded with less than a 20 per cent reduction. As has been stated previously, the technique is usually applied to bought-out items because it is in this group that the restrictions imposed by the method appear to be most valid. There are some inventory items for which the assumption that the ratio of ordering costs to holding costs remains constant irrespective of the number of replenishments per annum is definitely not valid. For instance inventory items at present having a low annual usage value, for which coverage analysis will more often than not recommend even fewer replenishments per year, could run an increased risk of obsolescence if this recommendation were put into effect.

Supporters of coverage analysis claim that although statistically it cannot be proved, the customer service levels remain overall much the same after the introduction of the method as before. However, by basing the calculation of replenishment order size on the same annual usage figure as experienced beforehand, the method does not take into account the interaction of replenishment order size and frequency of replenishment.

Despite these limitations, coverage analysis is a useful technique because it is simple to understand and, therefore, easy to apply in practice. Its main advantages can be summarised as follows:

(a) For the number of inventory items involved it is a very speedy method of analysis

(b) It produces a straightforward quantitative estimate of possible reductions in invested capital

(c) For the previous two reasons it is often more acceptable to management than more complicated techniques, even though these might effect marginally larger savings.

EXERCISES

No exercises are proposed for this chapter. It is suggested that readers wishing to apply the technique do so from a sample of their own inventory items.

REFERENCE

1. MURDOCH, J. (ed.), 'Coverage Analysis—A new technique for optimising the stock ordering policy', Proceedings of a one day conference held at Cranfield, (1965).

CHAPTER 10

Simulation of Inventory Situations

Presented with an inventory situation in which either or both the demand and leadtime distributions cannot be assumed to approximate to any specified mathematical distribution, the only method of analysis which can be used is that of 'simulation'.

As the name suggests, the technique of simulation is used to reproduce (usually in mathematical form) a typical series of situations which *could* well have occurred in practice. If enough of these situations are simulated and their mean value taken, it is assumed that this mean value represents what *would* most likely have happened in practice, had the real situation existed.

With the attempted mathematical analysis of more and more complicated industrial systems and the general availability of fast electronic computers, the 'art' of simulation has developed rapidly in the past decade. Special computer languages have been developed such as SIMSCRIPT and C.S.L. to make the programming of simulation problems on computers easier. Fortunately, however, for the computer simulation of simple inventory policy situations such sophisticated languages are not usually necessary, and the basic computer languages of the FORTRAN type are quite adequate.

GENERATION OF PSEUDO-RANDOM NUMBERS

To simulate a series of typical cases existing in an industrial inventory situation, it is first necessary to generate a series of what is hoped to be *typical* demand and leadtime values. These values and their corresponding probability of occurrence will presumably already be specified by past analysis as a probability distribution, and the method by which sample values are extracted from such a distribution to represent a typical situation will now be detailed.

To generate data suitable for simulation purposes from information held in probability distribution form, a source of 'pseudo-random numbers' must be available. These are drawn from a Uniform distribution and thus all numbers in the series have, theoretically, an equal probability of occurring. Such a series of random numbers is termed 'pseudo' because, as the numbers are generated artificially, statistically speaking the series is bound to repeat itself sometime. In practice, however, it is relatively simple to ensure that the pseudo-random number series does not repeat itself during a particular simulation run. For that run, therefore, the numbers can be considered as truly random.

Several sources of pseudo-random numbers are available for simulation purposes and some of these are described below:

(a) For simple manual simulation, sets of pseudo-random numbers can be obtained from mathematical tables.

(b) When using computer simulation, many computers have a special instruction or subroutine which automatically generates a series of pseudo-random numbers.

(c) A simple method of generating random numbers with an equal probability of occurrence between 00 and 99 is to take a two figure number, square it and take the two central numbers as the next random number and repeat:

Take 76, square is	5 776,	next random number is 77
77,	5 929,	92
92,	8 464,	46
46,	2 116,	11
11,	0 121,	12

The above method of generating pseudo-random numbers is known as the mid-square technique.

(*d*) Method (*c*) tends to break down for long simulation runs performed on a digital computer, so for such computer simulations more sophisticated methods such as the Lehmer Congruence, method should be used. This method and several others are described by Tocher,[1] who devotes a whole chapter of his book to the generation of pseudo-random numbers.

Having obtained a series of random numbers it is then quite simple to extract typical demand and leadtime values from their respective distributions. Consider the demand and leadtime distributions indicated in Tables 10.1 and 10.2. For the demand distribution it can be seen that the probability of a weekly demand value between 0 and 9 occurring is 10 per cent. It is apparent that if, for this example, a series

Table 10.1. DEMAND DISTRIBUTION

Demand per week, units	Class mid-point	Probability of occurrence, %	Allocated random number range
0– 9	4·5	10	1– 100
10–19	14·5	30	101– 400
20–29	24·5	30	401– 700
30–39	34·5	20	701– 900
40–50	44·5	5	901– 950
50 and above	54·5	5	951–1 000

Table 10.2. LEADTIME DISTRIBUTION

Leadtime duration, weeks	Probability of occurrence, %	Allocated random number range
1	5	1– 50
2	5	51– 100
3	30	101– 400
4	45	401– 850
5	10	851– 950
6, and longer	5	951–1 000

of random numbers between 1 and 1000 is generated with all numbers having an equal probability of occurring, then should those numbers between 1 and 100 be allocated to the 0 to 9 weekly demand class, the probability of that class of demand values occurring will also be 10 per cent. The numbers allocated to all other classes can be similarly arranged and the mid-point value of the class is usually taken as representing the whole class.

Thus a series of five random numbers 48, 560, 876, 849 and 251 would generate the weekly demand values 4·5, 24·5, 34·5, 34·5 and 14·5 units respectively or could be used to generate the following leadtime values: 1, 4, 5, 4 and 3 weeks.

SIMPLE MANUAL SIMULATION

To explain how a simulation of an inventory situation is executed, two manual simulations will first be considered. These are of a re-order level policy with a re-order level M of 100 units and a replenishment order quantity Q of 250 units, and of a re-order cycle policy with a review period of 12 weeks and a value of S of 300 units. These are presented in Tables 10.3 and 10.4. For both situations no back-ordering is allowed, and the demand per week and the leadtime durations to which the inventory systems are subjected are as in Tables 10.1 and 10.2. Both simulations last for a simulated year, that is for 48 weeks in this particular case, and the object of the simulation is to compare how well the two policies cope with the same demand and leadtime situation. To start the simulation, it is assumed for both policies that the inventory level is 150 units initially.

For the simulation of both inventory policies, a series of pseudo-random numbers (with one number for each week of the simulation except the first) must be derived from some source such as a table of such random number values. Having provided these random numbers, the corresponding values of the demand per week can be obtained from the demand distribution (in this case Table 10.1).

The procedure from now on is to treat the demand values as if they actually occurred in practice and to subtract them successively to form

Table 10.3. RE-ORDER LEVEL POLICY SIMULATION

Simulation period	Demand random number	Consequent weekly demand	Replenishment order situation	Lead-time random number	Lead-time remaining	Current inventory level	Number of replenishment orders placed	Number of weeks of stock-out
1	—	—	—	—	—	150·0	0	0
2	201	14·5	—	—	—	135·5	0	0
3	744	34·5	—	—	—	101·0	0	0
4	947	44·5	replenishment order for 250 placed	442	4	56·5*	1	0
5	221	14·5	outstanding	—	3	42·0	1	0
6	932	44·5	outstanding	—	2	0·0	1	1
7	450	24·5	outstanding	—	1	0·0	1	2
8	449	24·5	order of 250 received	—	0	225·5	1	2
9	162	14·5	—	—	—	211·0	1	2
10	45	4·5	—	—	—	206·5	1	2
11	327	14·5	—	—	—	192·0	1	2
12	36	4·5	—	—	—	187·5	1	2
13	624	24·5	—	—	—	163·0	1	2
14	610	24·5	—	—	—	138·5	1	2
15	890	34·5	—	—	—	104·0	1	2
16	17	4·5	replenishment order for 250 placed	56	2	99·5*	2	2
17	275	14·5	outstanding	—	1	85·0	2	2
18	490	24·5	order of 250 received	—	0	310·5	2	2
19	497	24·5	—	—	—	286·0	2	2
20	202	14·5	—	—	—	271·5	2	2
21	488	24·5	—	—	—	247·0	2	2
22	87	4·5	—	—	—	242·5	2	2
23	959	54·5	—	—	—	188·0	2	2
24	379	14·5	—	—	—	173·5	2	2
25	57	4·5	—	—	—	169·0	2	2
26	558	24·5	—	—	—	144·5	2	2
27	672	24·5	—	—	—	120·0	2	2
28	858	34·5	replenishment order for 250 placed	640	4	85·5*	3	2

(*Cont.* Table 10.3

Simu-lation period	De-mand random number	Conse-quent weekly demand	Replenishment order situation	Lead-time random number	Lead-time remain-ing	Current inventory level	Num-ber of reple-nish-ment orders placed	Numb er of week of stock out
29	401	24·5	outstanding	—	3	61·0	3	2
30	945	44·5	outstanding	—	2	16·5	3	2
31	116	14·5	outstanding	—	1	2·0	3	2
32	640	24·5	order of 250 received	—	0	227·5	3	2
33	509	24·5	—	—	—	203·0	3	2
34	669	24·5	—	—	—	178·5	3	2
35	335	14·5	—	—	—	164·0	3	2
36	524	24·5	—	—	—	139·5	3	2
37	749	34·5	—	—	—	105·0	3	2
38	502	24·5	replenishment order for 250 placed	171	3	80·5*	4	2
39	494	24·5	outstanding	—	2	56·0	4	2
40	196	14·5	outstanding	—	1	41·5	4	2
41	641	24·5	order of 250 received	—	0	267·0	4	2
42	184	14·5	—	—	—	252·5	4	2
43	655	24·5	—	—	—	228·0	4	2
44	799	34·5	—	—	—	193·5	4	2
45	72	4·5	—	—	—	189·0	4	2
46	900	34·5	—	—	—	154·5	4	2
47	538	24·5	—	—	—	130·0	4	2
48	981	54·5	—	—	—	75·5	4	2

Total   7 552·5

* (Note overshoot) ($M = 100$, $Q = 250$)

the current inventory level. If the current inventory level for the re-order level policy falls below 100 then a replenishment order for 250 units is placed. To determine how long the replenishment order will be delayed, another random number is generated and the corresponding leadtime evaluated from the leadtime distribution (in this case

Table 10.4. RE-ORDER CYCLE POLICY SIMULATION

Simu-lation period	De-mand random number	Conse-quent weekly demand	Replenishment order situation	Lead-time random number	Leadtime remaining	Re-view period remain-ing	Current inventory level	Number of reple-nish-ment orders placed	Numb-er of weeks of stock-out
1	—	—	—	—	—	5	150·0	0	0
2	21	4·5	—	—	—	4	145·5	0	0
3	115	14·5	—	—	—	3	131·0	0	0
4	408	24·5	—	—	—	2	106·5	0	0
5	151	14·5	—	—	—	1	92·0	0	0
6	505	24·5	replenishment order for 232·5 placed	153	3	0	67·5	1	0
7	698	24·5	outstanding	—	2	11	43·0	1	0
8	67	4·5	outstanding	—	1	10	38·5	1	0
9	278	14·5	order of 232·5 received	—	0	9	256·5	1	0
10	550	24·5	—	—	—	8	232·0	1	0
11	227	14·5	—	—	—	7	217·5	1	0
12	208	14·5	—	—	—	6	203·0	1	0
13	190	14·5	—	—	—	5	188·5	1	0
14	510	24·5	—	—	—	4	164·0	1	0
15	604	24·5	—	—	—	3	139·5	1	0
16	892	34·5	—	—	—	2	105·0	1	0
17	911	44·5	—	—	—	1	60·5	1	0
18	202	14·5	replenishment order for 254 placed	862	5	0	46·0	2	0
19	12	4·5	outstanding	—	4	11	41·5	2	0
20	476	24·5	outstanding	—	3	10	17·0	2	0
21	221	14·5	outstanding	—	2	9	2·5	2	0
22	52	4·5	outstanding	—	1	8	0·0	2	1
23	462	24·5	order of 254 received	—	0	7	229·5	2	1
24	243	14·5	—	—	—	6	215·0	2	1
25	234	14·5	—	—	—	5	200·5	2	1
26	413	24·5	—	—	—	4	176·0	2	1
27	492	24·5	—	—	—	3	151·5	2	1
28	738	34·5	—	—	—	2	117·0	2	1
29	582	24·5	—	—	—	1	92·5	2	1

Simulation period	Demand random number	Consequent weekly demand	Replenishment order situation	Leadtime random number	Leadtime remaining	Review period remaining	Current inventory level	Number of replenishment orders placed	Number of weeks of stock out
30	874	34·5	replenishment order for 242 placed	66	2	0	58·0	3	1
31	290	14·5	outstanding	—	1	11	43·5	3	1
32	684	24·5	order of 242 received	—	0	10	261·0	3	1
33	884	34·5	—	—	—	9	226·5	3	1
34	758	34·5	—	—	—	8	192·0	3	1
35	796	34·5	—	—	—	7	157·5	3	1
36	394	14·5	—	—	—	6	143·0	3	1
37	20	4·5	—	—	—	5	138·5	3	1
38	455	24·5	—	—	—	4	114·0	3	1
39	698	24·5	—	—	—	3	89·5	3	1
40	193	14·5	—	—	—	2	75·0	3	1
41	360	14·5	—	—	—	1	60·5	3	1
42	140	14·5	replenishment order for 254 placed	450	4	0	46·0	4	1
43	18	4·5	outstanding	—	3	11	41·5	4	1
44	668	24·5	outstanding	—	2	10	17·0	4	1
45	431	24·5	outstanding	—	1	9	0·0	4	2
46	204	14·5	order of 254 received	—	0	8	239·5	4	2
47	331	14·5	—	—	—	7	226·0	4	2
48	728	34·5	—	—	—	6	180·5	4	2
						Total	5 948·0		

($S = 300$, 12 week review period)

Table 10.2). This is considered as the leadtime remaining and for each succeeding week of the simulation it is reduced by one until no leadtime value remains, which indicates that the replenishment order is now available. For the particular week in which the leadtime expires and the replenishment order is received, the inventory level rises by the amount of the replenishment order less the demand for that particular week.

For the re-order cycle policy a count is kept of the number of weeks remaining in the 12 week review period, and when this time has expired a replenishment order is placed for an amount S (equal to 300 units) less the current inventory held at that time. The derivation of the lead-time associated with a particular replenishment order and its control concerning the receipt of that order is exactly the same as for the re-order level policy.

After running this manual simulation for both policies for a year, it can be seen that in both systems four replenishment orders were placed during the year and stockouts occurred during only two weeks of the same period. However, the aggregate inventory held for the re-order level for the year (7552·5 units) indicates that the average stock held for the year was 157·5 units as opposed to 124 for the re-order cycle policy (computed from the aggregate of 5948·0). Although the simulation period of a year is far too short to draw any positive conclusions (see discussion on length of simulation runs later) at first sight it would appear that the effect of these two particular policies with control parameters of the values stated, results in the same number of replenishment orders being placed and the same number of weeks of stockout occurring; but that the re-order cycle policy appears to be able to achieve these same conditions by holding far less inventory than the re-order level policy. Thus, if the unit cost of holding, ordering and stockouts are the same for the two policies (this need not necessarily be true) then because the total cost of holding is less for the re-order cycle policy than for the re-order level policy, the re-order cycle policy would appear to be the one to choose on a simple criterion of minimum cost.

LENGTH OF SIMULATION RUNS

A simulation run can be considered as a statistical sample of the process that one is trying to simulate; in other words just a section of an infinitely long simulation run. Considered thus, the information derived from simulation runs and the statistical confidence with which this information can be regarded will depend mainly on the length of the simulation run in the same way as the information derived from statistical sampling depends on the size of the sample taken.

The problem then is to determine how long the simulation run needs to be to estimate the desired variables of the system to a certain degree of accuracy with a desired degree of statistical confidence. The usual method for estimating the length of a simulation run is to perform a few short trial runs using different series of random numbers, and to find the mean and standard deviation of the variable that one is trying to measure, such as the average inventory level or the average number of stockouts. Knowing that the standard deviation of such a variable varies inversely as the square root of the length of the simulation run, it is possible to calculate approximately how long the final series of simulation runs needs to be to estimate the required variable with a stated degree of statistical confidence. In this situation one can usually assume that the measured variable is distributed normally.

To show how this method of calculating the length of computer runs could be applied in practice making this assumption two examples will be considered.

Example 1

In attempting to determine the average inventory level held when operating a particular re-order level policy, an initial series of simulation runs of ten years duration indicates that this average value is approximately 120 units with a standard deviation of 40 units. What minimum length of simulation runs would be required to specify this average inventory level value of 120 with an accuracy of ± 5 units and a statistical confidence of 95 per cent?

Solution. To specify a value to within ± 5 units with a 95 per cent confidence, the standard deviation σ_a must be less than or equal to the value evaluated as:

$$\sigma_a \leqslant 5/1 \cdot 6449$$

where 1·6449 is the value of the standard normal deviate at the 95 per cent level.

Therefore:

$$\sigma_a \leqslant 3·04$$

Now as the standard deviation of a variable within a simulation run is inversely proportional to the square root of the length of the run,

$$\frac{\sigma_a}{40} \doteqdot \sqrt{\frac{10}{N}}$$

where N is the desired run length in years.

Thus N the answer $\doteqdot \dfrac{10 \times 40^2}{(3·04)^2} = 1\,740$ years or more.

Example 2

If it were possible for the previous problem to have a simulation run length of only 1 000 years, how accurately could the average be estimated with 95 per cent confidence?

Solution. For a 1 000 years simulation run length, σ_a is given by

$$\sigma_a \doteqdot 40 \times \sqrt{\frac{10}{1\,000}} = 4$$

Therefore, the accuracy of estimating the average inventory level would be given by $\pm 4 \times 1·6449 = \pm 6·6$ units.

COMPUTER SIMULATION OF INVENTORY SYSTEMS

The two simulation examples just considered indicate why in all practical circumstances, to predict reasonably accurately with any degree of statistical confidence, simulation runs become so long that computer simulation is essential. The simulation of 1 740 years represents

83 520 weekly calculations (at 48 weeks to the year) and this is obviously out of the question for manual simulation when a computer can perform this series of calculations in a matter of a few seconds. The writing of inventory simulation computer program is a relatively simple matter for anyone familiar with a basic computer language such as FORTRAN and a typical block diagram for the simulation of a re-order level policy with no backordering allowed is shown in Fig. 10.1. To understand more fully the workings of this block diagram it is suggested that, starting at Block *a*, readers trace through the system to see what happens after the current demand has been subtracted from the immediate past inventory level, and the current inventory level is:

(*a*) Still above the re-order level
(*b*) Below the re-order level for the first time (i.e. the immediate past inventory level was above the re-order level)
(*c*) Below the re-order level but with the leadtime only partially expired
(*d*) Zero, and the leadtime remaining is zero also.

The routings taken by each of these situations through the various logic blocks (which are identified alphabetically) are indicated at the beginning of the Exercise examples at the end of this chapter.

To illustrate computer simulation of inventory systems further to the reader, several recordings of a simulation of the re-order level, re-order cycle and the (*s*, *S*) policies are shown as Figs. 10.2, 10.3 and 10.4. It should be pointed out that the computer output illustrated here is not typical of a digital computer output and has been obtained by a rather special method (see Lewis[2]). This type of display of output recordings does have the advantage however of being very similar in form to the conventional inventory balance diagrams and can, therefore, be more easily contrasted with such diagrams.

In Fig. 10.2 recordings of the inventory levels obtained for a re-order level policy over a period of about 100 simulation periods can be seen to be very similar in form to the familiar inventory balance diagram. In addition, however, at the bottom of the diagram are pulses whose heights represent the size of replenishment orders

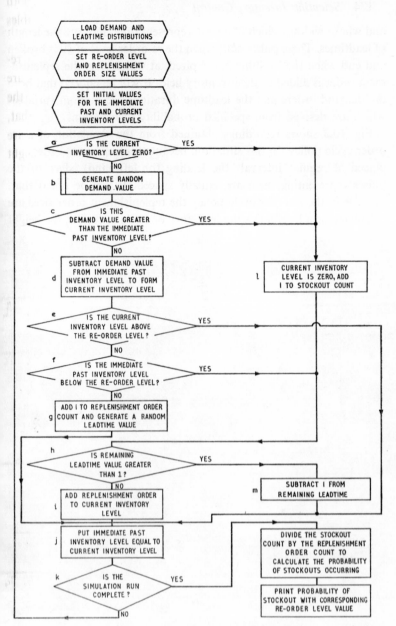

Fig. 10.1. Block diagram of a computer program required to simulate a re-order level policy and calculate probability of stockouts

and whose widths (which of course represent time) indicate the length of leadtimes. These pulses start when the re-order level of 40 is broken and end when the leadtime has expired, at which time the replenishment order is added to the inventory held. It will be noticed that both the demand orders and the leadtime durations are random variables which are derived from specified probability distributions.

Fig. 10.3 shows recordings obtained from the simulation of a re-order cycle policy. In this situation, because replenishment orders are placed at regular intervals the leading (or left-hand) edges of the pulses representing them are equally spaced. It will be noted that, because in the re-order cycle policy the replenishment order sizes are calculated as a level S less the inventory on hand at review, the height

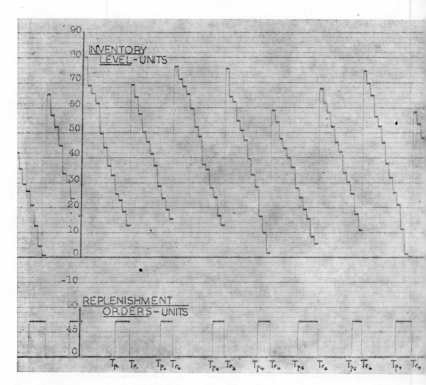

Fig. 10.2. Re-order level policy. Unlimited store size, backordering prohibited

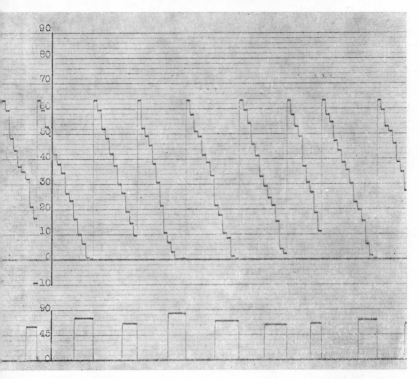

Fig. 10.3. Re-order cycle policy. Limited store size, backordering prohibited

of pulses representing these order sizes vary considerably, whereas in the previous recording of the re-order level policy these remained fixed. For the recordings taken from the simulation of an (s, S) policy (Fig. 10.4), review times at which no replenishment order was placed because the inventory held at that time was above s are indicated as 'A'. In the particular situation illustrated here this non-placing of orders has resulted in both cases in a subsequent stockout, and consequently very large replenishment orders being placed at the next review.

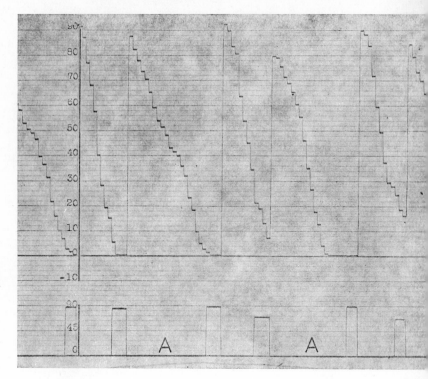

Fig. 10.4. s, S policy (S = 42). Unlimited store size, backordering prohibited

ASSESSING INVENTORY OPERATING COSTS
FROM SIMULATION

If one considers that the total inventory operating costs are made up of: the cost of holding stock; the cost of ordering replenishment orders; and the cost involved in running out of stock, it is relatively simple with a computer simulation model to evaluate the assumed inventory operating costs per simulation run. Fortunately, although computer simulation runs tend to be very long, the capacity of the modern computer is such that extremely large numbers can be stored for accumulation purposes during the computer run. Most computers can cope with a number of up to eleven significant figures and several have a facility for storing 'double length numbers' and thus even extending this range. The reason for this accumulation facility will become evident during the discussion on the evaluation of the individual constituent costs.

Cost of holding stock

This is usually associated with the average level of inventory held. In a computer simulation run this average level can be evaluated by accumulating (i.e. adding to the previous summed total as in the manual simulation mentioned earlier in the chapter) the current inventory level for *every* time period of the simulation run. By dividing the final accumulated value by the number of time units in the simulation run, the average inventory level can be found. Knowing the average inventory level and the unit cost of holding, the actual holding cost is evaluated as the product of the two.

Cost of replenishment

Knowing the number of replenishment orders placed during a simulation run, the cost of replenishment is obviously this number times the cost for a single replenishment.

Cost of stockout

If it is assumed that a fixed cost is incurred every time a stockout occurs, the total cost is the product of the number of stockouts that occur during the simulation run and the cost of an individual stockout. If, however, the cost of stockout is assumed to be proportional to the length of time that a stockout situation exists, the number of simulation periods when stockout occurs should be accumulated and the cost evaluated from this figure.

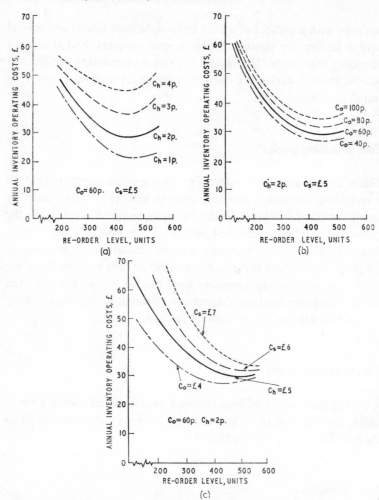

*Fig. 10.5. Cost of operating a re-order level policy for differing constituent cos^t
conditions (Q = 600 units)*
(a) differing holding costs, (b) differing ordering costs, (c) differing stockout costs

Figs. 10.5 and 10.6 show inventory operating costs as evaluated
from a computer simulation for the situation where a re-order level
policy and a re-order cycle policy are used respectively to control
the same demand and leadtime situation with the same assumed costs
of ordering, holding and replenishment. For both situations four

different assumed values for each constituent cost are used while the remaining two are kept constant. This technique is used to investigate the sensitivity of the simulation model to differences in the constituent

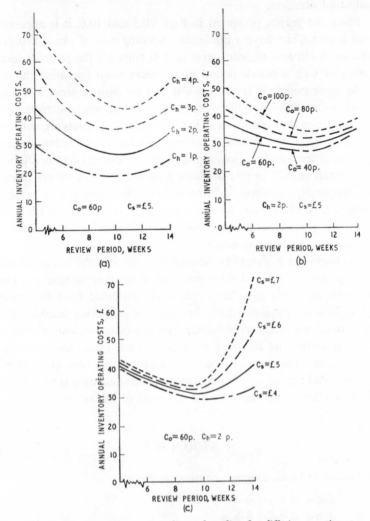

Fig. 10.6. Costs of operating a re-order cycle policy for differing constituent cost conditions (S = 1 000 units) (a) differing holding costs, (b) differing ordering costs, (c) differing stockout costs

costs. It should be noted that generally, corresponding constituent costs need not necessarily be the same for different types of policy even when dealing with the same demand and leadtime data in the same industrial situation.

From the graphs presented in Figs. 10.5 and 10.6, it is apparent that both policies have a minimum operating cost of about £30 per annum at either a re-order level of 450 units for the re-order level policy or with a review period of 10 weeks when operating the re-order cycle policy. It is also evident that for high re-order levels or short review periods, differences in the costs of stockout have very little effect on the overall cost as in this situation stockouts are unlikely to occur very often. Similarly, for low re-order levels and long review periods differences in ordering costs have a reduced effect in altering the overall cost as in this situation replenishment orders are placed less frequently. However, differences in holding costs appear to have considerable effect over the whole range investigated, indicating the relative importance of holding compared with ordering replenishments or allowing stockouts to occur.

In conclusion it should be realised that this chapter has presented a very much simplified description of simulation techniques. The methods described have been specifically extracted from the much wider field of simulation with the object of producing feasible solutions to certain inventory problems. Simulation as a technique is much more versatile (and therefore more complicated) than has been suggested here. The general field of simulation has been covered by Tocher[1] and the use of computer methods in simulation is to be dealt with by Clementson[3] in a companion issue of this series.

EXERCISES

Solutions to block diagram routing problem:

- i.   a–b–c–d–e–j–k–a–
- ii. a–b–c–d–e–f–g–j–k–a–
- iii. a–b–c–d–e–f–h–m–j–k–a–
- iv. a–e–h–i–j–k–a–

1. Using the random numbers in Table 10.3, simulate a year's operation of the re-order cycle policy, and using the random numbers in Table 10.4 simulate a year's operation of the re-order level policy

2. If a variable measured by simulation can be estimated with a certain accuracy with a 95 per cent statistical confidence by a series of simulation runs 10 000 periods long; with what confidence can this accuracy be maintained for a series of simulation runs of only 7 000 periods duration?

Answer. 91·6 per cent confidence

3. If it is required to estimate a system variable to within ±5 per cent accuracy with a 95 per cent degree of statistical confidence, what length of computer run is required if a series of runs 750 periods long indicate that the standard deviation is 18 per cent?

Answer. 26 500 periods approximately

4. For the previous example, what length of computer run would be required to improve the statistical confidence of prediction to 98 per cent still maintaining the same accuracy?

Answer. 40 000 periods approximately

REFERENCES

1. TOCHER, K. D., *The Art of Simulation*, English Universities Press, London (1963).
2. LEWIS, C. D., 'Hybrid-analog Simulation of Stochastic Industrial Storage Problems', *J. Ind. Engng*, **18**, No. 4, 260 (1967).
3. CLEMENTSON, A. T. *Techniques of Computer Simulation*, Butterworths, London, (manuscript in preparation).

Sources of Random Number Tables

FISHER, R. A. and YATES, F., *Statistical Tables*, Oliver and Boyd, Edinburgh (1948).
LINDLEY, D. V. and MILLER, J. C. P., *Cambridge Elementary Statistical Tables*, Cambridge University Press (1961).
THE RAND CORPORATION, *One Million Random Digits and* 100 000 *Normal Deviates*, The Free Press—Glencoe; Illinois (1955).

CHAPTER 11

A General Approach to Inventory Control Problems

Preceding chapters have dealt with specific methods and models used in implementing inventory control theory into practical methods of stock control. In this chapter a more general approach will be taken to the problems of carrying out the theory.

The inventory control considerations of a company can most easily be identified on a basis of time as long-term, intermediate or short-term plans, and emergency procedures.

LONG-TERM INVENTORY PLANS

Because inventories represent a large portion of a company's invested capital, any long-term plans involving inventory will naturally be closely associated with any future capital investment policy. Fluctuations in interest rates and any other legislation which influences capital would, therefore, be expected also to control investment in stocks. As stocks are held primarily to meet customer demand, long-term predictions of demand will often be necessary to formulate a company's future plans on invested capital and thus, investment in inventory. Although many imponderables can influence long-term predictions and thus reduce their accuracy, a technique that has been used by more sophisticated managements in an endeavour to produce a long-term sales pattern is that of multiple linear regression. This technique, which is fully described by Ferber,[1] has been used in an attempt to associate a company's long-term growth of sales with certain relevant published statistics and also to try to quantify that degree of association. A recent study of a company marketing measuring equipment has indicated that its sales were highly correlated with a combination of three nationally published statistics concerning exports. Here the degree of correlation, that is the ratio of the variance explained by the regression technique compared with the overall variance, was as high as 80 per cent. Care must of course be taken when using regression analysis to ensure that the statistics used are relevant, but used intelligently this technique can improve the accuracy of long-term prediction of sales at company level.

INTERMEDIATE AND SHORT-TERM PLANS

It is at this level of inventory policy planning that the bulk of what inventory control theory has to offer can and should be used. It is at this level that the day-to-day running of the stock control system must be matched with the company's overall directives concerning inventory. The day-to-day running of the stock control system is usually based on one of many standardised paperwork procedures which have been developed over the years, and excellent coverage of most of these will be found in such books as those by Burbidge,[2] Buffa,[3] Eilon[4] and Carroll.[5]

When deciding on which specific stock control system to use, items must generally be grouped together rather than considered individually to ensure that the administrative effort required to effect control does not become prohibitive. Several methods of grouping are possible, the most familiar being perhaps the *ABC* value analysis method which, like the method of coverage analysis groups on an annual usage value basis. Unlike coverage analysis, however, *ABC* value analysis concentrates all stocked items into three uneven classes and

not into a dozen or so equal classes. The reason for this type of grouping is that in many companies it has been shown that a large proportion of the usage or sales value of stocked items is concentrated in
only relatively few of those items. If, therefore, the percentage of the
value of annual usage is plotted against the proportion of stocked
items which go to make up that value, a typical curve which often can
occur is as shown in Fig. 11.1. Here it can be seen that only 10 per cent

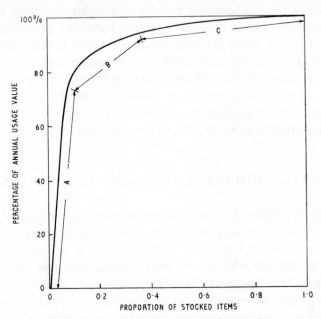

Fig. 11.1. Distribution of annual usage value with proportion of stocked items

of the stocked items make up 80 per cent of the value of annual usage,
a further 30 per cent contribute about 15 per cent and the remaining
60 per cent of stocked items contribute a mere 5 per cent. These three
classes based on annual usage value are labelled for convenience *A*, *B*
and *C*. *A* items are those of high value which would require a strict
method of stock control and thus a fairly sophisticated method of
forecasting with perhaps some form of demand monitoring. *B* items
are of the middle range value requiring a slightly less strict method of

stock control which might, therefore, be combined with an adaptive response rate method of forecasting. *C* items, representing the most numerous but the cheapest items such as nuts, bolts, washers, etc., would require the simplest form of stock control such as the Two-Bin method or one of its variants. In some cases it may not even be necessary to maintain formal stock records of such items, as the cost involved in doing so would be of the same order as the material cost of the item. However, if such a method is introduced, it is usual to instigate some method of random checking to avoid losses due to carelessness and perhaps pilfering.

Other inventory classification systems have been based on such variables as an item's turnover value (indicating active and sluggish stocked parts) or on a system which designates the use of the stocked part, such as 'general materials', 'common parts', etc. With all these methods of grouping, however, the main purpose is to indicate the order of importance of individual stock items. This enables them to be controlled collectively within their group classification with methods which can be arranged to become progressively less exacting and less expensive to operate as the importance of the items in each class declines.

Of the various tools available for calculating parameters of inventory control systems, the slide-rule, the nomogram and the digital computer are the most important. These devices obviously have applications in many other fields as well but their particular usefulness when applied to inventory control will be discussed briefly here.

The Slide-Rule

Familiar to most engineers, this rule composed of two sliding sections and a cursor, can be used to multiply, divide and to evaluate square root values. This latter feature is particularly useful in calculating inventory control parameters, but the skill required to use the slide-rule appears to be just a little too high for it to become universally popular for work in this field.

The Nomogram

This is a special type of graph which can be used for calculating the answers to specific equations. Based on similar principles to the slide-rule it too can be used for multiplying, dividing and evaluating square root values. However, the skill required for its use is not as high as that needed for a slide-rule. An example of its simplicity is illustrated

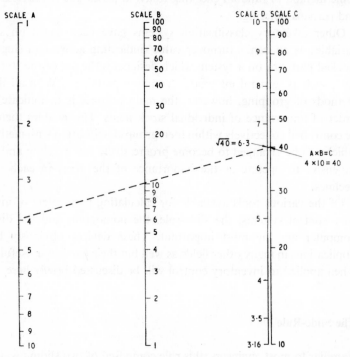

Fig. 11.2. Nomogram for multiplying two variables and evaluating the square root of the product

in Fig. 11.2 which demonstrates a simple multiplication with the option of evaluating either the product of two variables or the square root of the product. The problem given is to evaluate the result of the multiplication of 4 times 10 and in addition to find the square root of that result. By drawing a straight line through the position 4 on scale *A* and position 10 on scale *B*, the resultant product 40 can be read directly from scale *C*, and the square root of the product 6·3 can also be read directly on scale *D*. A further example has already been demonstrated by the nomogram in Fig. 2.1, used for calculating forecasts based on simple exponentially weighted averages.

Because they are easy to use, nomograms have been applied extensively to inventory control calculations. Buchan and Koenigsberg[6] have devoted a whole chapter of their book to the construction of nomograms specifically for inventory control, and the design and construction of nomograms for all classes of computation in industry have been detailed by Allcock *et al.*[1]

The Digital Computer

Over the last decade this has been used increasingly in controlling stocked items. Although its accuracy is usually embarrassingly high for most stock control problems, it is the digital computer's speed of sorting and ability to store large amounts of information relatively cheaply that have made it such a useful tool in this field.

The digital computer is such a versatile device that it is more than probable that many applications for which it is suited in inventory control have yet to be explored. Perhaps one of the greatest factors holding back such developments is the lack of understanding of the computer as a completely new medium for the storage and manipulation of data. Thus the approach has generally been to use the computer simply to do what was previously done either manually or by punched card sorting methods rather than to design the system completely around the computer's own special characteristics.

EMERGENCY PROCEDURES

All the inventory models considered so far in this book have been concerned with *typical* demand situations as represented by average values of central tendency (i.e. the mean or average) or of deviation

13*

about that central value (i.e. the standard deviation or the mean absolute deviation). As one would expect, these models based on average demand values do not react at all well when presented with *untypical* demand situations. Such a situation can readily be identified in the large, on-off demand order which is never likely to be repeated.

Some questions posed by this type of problem could be:

What type of response should one expect from an inventory control system subject to such a single period demand impulse? Is it reasonable to expect any control system to cope satisfactorily with such untypical demand situations?

Consider the two different responses to a single period demand impulse as depicted in Fig. 11.3 and 11.4. In the situation represented in Fig. 11.3 in which the control system does not respond at all, the sum of squared errors is represented simply by a^2, where a is the error generated at the time the demand impulse occurred. In the situation represented in Fig. 11.4 however (which is typical of an exponentially weighted average type of response) because the attempted response is one period late, a maximum error value a is again formed at the instant the single period demand impulse occurs. In addition, however, subsequent errors b, c, d and e are also formed due to the lagged response.

Although these errors are negative in character compared with the first error a, they still contribute to the sum of squared forecasting errors which then becomes $a^2 + b^2 + c^2 + d^2 + e^2$.

From this very brief inspection, it would appear that ideally a control system based on average values (and thus by inference typical demand situations) should ignore completely sudden short upsurges in demand. If this naïve hypothesis is accepted one is still presented with two problems, namely, identification and fulfillment of the sudden demand impulse.

To identify a demand impulse and distinguish it from a step in demand (which will initially appear the same), one will have to rely mainly on market intelligence. Aids such as Trigg's tracking signal and Cusum monitoring methods can identify when a sudden increase in demand occurs, but they cannot indicate whether this new demand level is likely to be sustained or not. It is obviously essential to be able

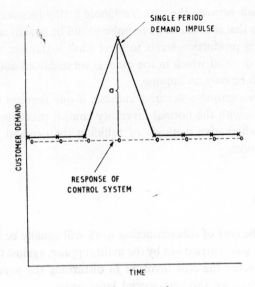

Fig. 11.3. Control system with no response

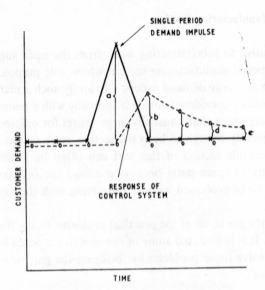

Fig. 11.4. Control system with exponentially weighted average type of response

to distinguish between the two. To ignore a step increase in demand on the basis that it could be an impulse would be equally as disastrous as increasing production levels to meet what is thought to be a step increase in demand which in the event is not sustained and eventually turns out to be only an impulse.

Having recognised a demand impulse, if one requires that it does not interfere with the normal inventory control procedure, there are two main alternative methods of fulfilling the demand represented by that impulse.

Subcontract

Although the cost of subcontracting work will usually be higher than if that work were carried out by the main supplier, against this increase can be deducted the cost involved in disturbing the normal control system to produce this one special large order.

One-off Manufacturing Section

An alternative to subcontracting work from the main supplier, is to set up a special manufacturing section whose sole purpose is to deal with unusually large demand orders. Obviously such a manufacturing section could be considered only in a company with a reasonably wide product range such that unusually large orders for different products occur frequently enough to keep the section more or less fully occupied. A versatile section of this sort can often be justified for the manufacture of spare parts because it allows the occasional orders for spares to be processed without interfering with the main production effort.

These then are some of the practical problems facing the inventory controller. It is hoped that some of the models proposed in this book may help solve those problems by 'bridging the gap between theory and practice'.

REFERENCES

1. FERBER, R., *Statistical Techniques in Market Research*, McGraw-Hill, New York (1949).
2. BURBIDGE, J. L., *The Principles and Practice of Production Control*, Macdonald and Evans, London (1962).
3. BUFFA, E. S., *Modern Production Management*, John Wiley, New York (1961).
4. EILON, S., *Element of Production Planning and Inventory Control*, Macmillan, New York (1962).
5. CARROLL, P., *Practical Production and Inventory Control*, McGraw-Hill, New York (1966).
6. BUCHAN, J. and KOENIGSBERG, E., *Scientific Inventory Management*, Prentice-Hall, Englewood Cliffs (1963).
7. ALLCOCK, H. J., JONES, J. R. and MICHEL, J. G. L., *The Nomogram*, Pitman and Sons, London (1962).

Glossary

A	Annual demand, usage or sales turnover
a	A constant
b	A constant
b	When subscripted represents the demand growth factor
C	A general cost parameter: usually represents annual inventory operating costs
C'	Annual inventory operating cost for capital restriction situation
C^*	Annual inventory operating cost for aggregate total set-up time limitation situation
C_a	Unit selling price
C_h	Unit holding cost (often equated as iC_n)
C_m	Work's prime or material and labour cost
C_s	Stockout cost
C_o	Cost of placing a replenishment order, or the set-up cost involved in initiating a production run
$\bar{D}$	Average demand per unit time
d	When used as a subscript indicates appertaining to demand
e	Forecasting error
$\bar{e}$	Exponentially weighted average of forecasting errors
F	Probability of a stockout
F	When subscripted represents the smoothed de-seasonalising factor
f	Annual frequency of stockouts
G	Inventory coverage
g	Normalising factor
I	Average inventory level
i	Holding charge interest rate
j	Used only as a subscript and then indicates appertaining to the jth item
K	Number of time periods in a seasonal cycle
$\bar{K}$	Average overshoot of the re-order level
k	Standard normal deviate
k_o	Modified standard normal deviate
k^*	Optimal standard normal deviate for joint calculation method
L	Average leadtime duration

l	When used as a subscript indicates appertaining to the leadtime
M	Re-order level
m	Number of reviews or replenishments per year
m	Mean absolute deviation when subscripted
N	Number of items in a class or group
N	Length of a simulation run in time periods
n	Number of periods covered by a moving average
n	Arrivals in a time interval t
$\bar{n}$	Average number of queue members
P	Customer service level
P	When subscripted indicates probability of occurrence
q, Q	General replenishment order quantity
Q_o	Economic order quantity
$Q_{30°}$	Minimum economic order quantity
$Q_{45°}$	Minimum economic order quantity
Q'_o, Q''_o, Q^*_o	Modified economic order quantities
q^*	Optimal replenishment order quantity for joint calculation method
R	Review period
r	A general variable
S	Maximum inventory level from which replenishment orders are calculated
S	Average total storage space
s	Level above which replenishment orders are not placed at review
T	Annual aggregate set-up time limit
T	Trigg's tracking signal when subscripted with t
t	When used as a subscript indicates time period
t	When subscripted represents set-up time
u	Exponentially weighted average of demand
$\bar{u}$	Adaptive response rate exponentially weighted average of demand
W	Storage space required per item
x	Percentage variation of annual usage rate
y	Demand in unit time period indicated by subscript
$\hat{y}$	Forecast of demand for subscripted time period
Z	Constant of proportionality
z	Lagrange multiplier
α	Exponential smoothing constant ($0 < \alpha < 1$)
β	Exponential smoothing constant ($0 < \beta < 1$)
γ	Exponential smoothing constant ($0 < \gamma < 1$)
δ	Small increment
λ	Average arrival rate
θ	Lagrange multiplier
ϱ	Traffic intensity
μ	Reciprocal of mean service time
σ	Standard deviation
Σ	Summation sign
τ	Average time between demands
ϕ	Probability of a machine failure
ψ	Lagrange multiplier

Appendix A. Summary of Equations

CHAPTER 2

Exponential progression

$$\alpha + \alpha(1-\alpha) + \alpha(1-\alpha)^2 + \ldots = 1 \tag{2-1}$$

Exponentially weighted average

$$u_t = \alpha y_t + (1-\alpha)u_{t-1} \tag{2-2}$$

Forecast for stationary demand distribution

$$\hat{y}_{t+T} = u_t \tag{2-3}$$

Growth factor for non-stationary demand distribution

$$b_t = \beta(u_t - u_{t-1}) + (1-\beta)b_{t-1} \tag{2-4}$$

Forecast for non-stationary demand distribution

$$\hat{y}_{t+T} = u_t + b_t T \tag{2-5}$$

Exponentially weighted average for seasonal demand situation

$$u_t = \frac{\alpha y_t}{F_{t-K}} + (1-\alpha)(u_{t-1} + b_{t-1}) \tag{2-6}$$

De-seasonalising factor for seasonal cycle of K periods

$$F_t = \frac{\gamma y_t}{u_t} + (1-\gamma)F_{t-K} \tag{2-7}$$

Growth factor for seasonal demand situation

$$b_t = \beta(u_t - u_{t-1}) + (1-\beta)b_{t-1} \tag{2-8}$$

Forecast for seasonal demand situation

$$\hat{y}_{t+T} = (u_t + b_t T)F_{t-K+T} \tag{2-9}$$

Forecasting error
$$e_t = y_t - \hat{y}_t \tag{2-10}$$

Mean absolute deviation of forecasting errors
$$m_t = \alpha \, |e_t| + (1-\alpha)m_{t-1} \tag{2-11}$$

Estimate of standard deviation of forecasting errors
$$\sigma_t = 1 \cdot 25 m_t \tag{2-12}$$

Exponentially weighted average of forecasting errors
$$\bar{e}_t = \alpha e_t + (1-\alpha)\bar{e}_{t-1} \tag{2-13}$$

Trigg's tracking signal
$$T_t = \bar{e}_t / m_t \tag{2-14}$$

CONFIDENCE LIMITS FOR TRIGG'S TRACKING SIGNAL

Cumulative	T_t	
probability, %	$\alpha = 0 \cdot 1$	$\alpha = 0 \cdot 2$
0	0·0	0·0
50	0·21	0·32
70	0·30	0·46
80	0·36	0·54
90	0·45	0·66
95	0·51	0·74
100	1·00	1·00

Adaptive response rate forecast
$$\hat{y}_{t+T} = \bar{u}_t = |T_t| \, y_t + (1 - |T_t|)\bar{u}_{t-1} \tag{2-15}$$

Modified adaptive response rate forecast
(Avoids spurious response to single period demand impulses)
$$\hat{y}_{t+T} = \bar{u}_t = |T_{t-1}| \, y_t + (1 - |T_{t-1}|)\bar{u}_{t-1} \tag{2-16}$$

CHAPTER 3

Re-order level for Normally distributed demand and fixed leadtimes
$$M = \bar{D}\bar{L} + k\sigma_d \sqrt{L} \tag{3-1}$$

Standard Normal deviate from (3.1)
$$k = \frac{M - \bar{D}\bar{L}}{\sigma_d \sqrt{L}} \tag{3-2}$$

Re-order level for uncorrelated, normally distributed demand and leadtimes

$$M = \bar{D}\bar{L} + k \sqrt{(\bar{L}\sigma_d^2 + \bar{D}^2\sigma_l^2)} \tag{3-3}$$

Standard normal deviate from (3.3)

$$k = \frac{M - \bar{D}\bar{L}}{\sqrt{(\bar{L}\sigma_d^2 + \bar{D}^2\sigma_l^2)}} \tag{3-4}$$

Modified re-order level for variable leadtimes

$$M = \bar{D}\bar{L} + k_o\sigma_d\sqrt{\bar{L}} \tag{3-5}$$

where

L	1	2	3	4	5	6	7	8
k_0	$1\cdot1k$	$1\cdot1k$	$1\cdot2k$	$1\cdot2k$	$1\cdot3k$	$1\cdot3k$	$1\cdot4k$	$1\cdot4k$

Average overshoot

$$\bar{K} = \tfrac{1}{2}(\bar{D} - 1 + \sigma_d^2/\bar{D}) \tag{3-6}$$

Total annual cost

$$C = \frac{C_oA}{q} + (M - \bar{D}\bar{L} + q/2)C_h \tag{3-7}$$

Economic order quantity

$$Q_o = \sqrt{\frac{2C_oA}{C_h}} \tag{3-8}$$

Economic order quantity with percentage holding cost

$$Q_o = \sqrt{\frac{2C_oA}{iC_m}} \tag{3-9}$$

Minimum economic order quantity (30°)

$$Q_{30°} = \sqrt{\frac{2\sqrt{3}C_oA}{\sqrt{3}C_h + 2}} \tag{3-10}$$

Minimum economic order quantity (45°)

$$Q_{45°} = \sqrt{\frac{2C_oA}{C_h + 2}} \tag{3-11}$$

Maximum profit order quantity

$$Q_p = \frac{C_a - C_m}{2C_o}Q_o^2 \tag{3-12}$$

Sensitivity of annual cost to inaccurate forecasts

$$C^1/C = \tfrac{1}{2}[\sqrt{(1 + x/100)} + 1/\sqrt{(1 + x/100)}] \tag{3-13}$$

for values see Table 3.8, p. 67.

CHAPTER 4

Linear logarithmic approximation for relating probability of stockout and safety stock

$$\log_e F = a - bk \tag{4-1}$$

$$F = e^{a-bk} \tag{4-2}$$

Total annual inventory operating cost based on above

$$C = \frac{AC_s e^{a-bk}}{100q} + \frac{AC_o}{q} + \frac{qC_h}{2} + k\sigma_d \sqrt{L} C_h \tag{4-3}$$

Optimum order quantity

$$q^* = \frac{\sigma_d \sqrt{L}}{b} + \sqrt{\left(\frac{\sigma_d^2 L}{b^2} + \frac{2AC_o}{C_h}\right)} \tag{4-4}$$

Optimum number of standard deviations of demand during the leadtime used as safety stock

$$k^* = \frac{1}{b} \left[a - \frac{\log_e 100\sigma_d \sqrt{L} C_h q^*}{bC_s A} \right] \tag{4-5}$$

Re-order level using above

$$M = \bar{D}\bar{L} + k^* \sigma_d \sqrt{L} \tag{4-6}$$

Proportion of demands met immediately ex-stock

$$G(M, Q) = \sum_{r=0}^{r=M} p_{\bar{L}}(r) + \frac{1}{Q} \sum_{r=M+1}^{r=M+Q} (M+Q-r)\, p_{\bar{L}}(r) \tag{4-7}$$

Average number of item months of shortage per annum

$$B(M, Q) = 12 \left[\sum_{r=0}^{r=M} \left(M + \frac{Q+1}{2} - r\right) p_{\bar{L}}(r) \right.$$
$$\left. + \frac{1}{2Q} \sum_{r=M+1}^{r=M+Q} (M+Q+1-r)(M+Q-r)\, p_L(r) - \left(M + \frac{Q+1}{2} - \bar{D}\bar{L}\right) \right] \tag{4-8}$$

Criteria for determining M when cost per item month of stock shortage (Z) is known

$$G(M, Q) < \frac{Z}{12C_m i + Z} \tag{4-9}$$

CHAPTER 5

Inventory operating costs when m reviews per year

$$C = \frac{A}{2m} C_h + mC_o \tag{5-1}$$

Economic number of reviews per year

$$m = \sqrt{\frac{AC_h}{2C_o}} \qquad (5\text{-}2)$$

Calculation of maximum inventory level S for a re-order cycle policy

$$S = \bar{D}(R+\bar{L}) + k\sigma_d \sqrt{(R+\bar{L})} \qquad (5\text{-}3)$$

Annual frequency of stockout for a re-order cycle policy

$$f = \frac{100-P}{2R} \qquad (5\text{-}4)$$

Value of re-order level when policy is subject to periodic reviews

$$M = \bar{D}(R/2+\bar{L}) + k\sigma_d \sqrt{(R/2+\bar{L})} \qquad (5\text{-}5)$$

Equating E.O.Q. with average expected usage in an (s, S) policy

$$Q_o = \sqrt{\frac{2AC_o}{C_h}} = S - s + \frac{A}{2} \times \frac{R}{50} \qquad (5\text{-}6)$$

Resultant value of maximum inventory level S

$$S = \sqrt{\frac{2AC_o}{C_h}} - s + \frac{AR}{100} \qquad (5\text{-}7)$$

CHAPTER 6

Definition of Poissonian distribution of arrivals

$$P(n) = \frac{(\lambda t)^n e^{-\lambda t}}{n!} \qquad (6\text{-}1)$$

Probability of exactly n queue members

$$P_n = \varrho^n P_0 \qquad (6\text{-}2)$$

or

$$P_n = \varrho^n(1-\varrho) \qquad (6\text{-}3)$$

Average number of all queue members

$$\bar{n} = \frac{\varrho}{1-\varrho} \qquad (6\text{-}4)$$

Average number of queue members waiting for service

$$\bar{q} = \frac{\varrho^2}{1-\varrho} \qquad (6\text{-}5)$$

Average delay caused by the queue

$$\bar{t} = \frac{\bar{n}}{\mu} = \frac{1}{\mu} \frac{\varrho}{1-\varrho} \qquad (6\text{-}6)$$

Traffic intensity for two stage synchronous buffer stock situation

$$\varrho = \frac{\phi_2(1-\phi_1)}{\phi_1(1-\phi_2)} \tag{6-7}$$

Probability of no buffer stock

$$P_o(t) = 1-\varrho = \frac{\phi_1-\phi_2}{\phi_1(1-\phi_2)} \tag{6-8}$$

Probability of generated output

$$P_{\text{out}} = 1-\phi_1 \tag{6-9}$$

CHAPTER 7

Definition of Poissonian probability of breakdown

$$P(n) = \frac{(\bar{L}/\tau)^n \, e^{-\bar{L}/\tau}}{n!} \tag{7-1}$$

Average annual cost of keeping spare parts

$$C_N = iCp\left[N-\frac{L}{\tau}\left\{\sum_{n=0}^{N-1} P(n)\middle/ \sum_{n=0}^{N} P(n)\right\}\right]$$

$$+\frac{C_s}{\tau}\left\{P(N)\middle/ \sum_{n=0}^{N} P(n)\right\} + \frac{C_o}{\tau}\left\{1-P(N)\middle/ \sum_{n=0}^{N} P(n)\right\} \tag{7-2}$$

CHAPTER 8

Average total value invested in stocks

$$V = g \sum_{j=1}^{J} q_j C_{m_j} \tag{8-1}$$

Capital restriction

$$V_{\max}-g \sum_{j=1}^{J} q_j C_{m_j} \geqslant 0 \tag{8-2}$$

Annual inventory operating cost

$$C = \sum_{j=1}^{J}\left\{\frac{C_{oj}A_j}{q_j}+\frac{q_j C_{mj}i}{2}\right\} + z\left\{V_{\max}-g \sum_{j=1}^{J} q_j C_{m_j}\right\} \tag{8-3}$$

Modified economic order quantity when a capital limitation is imposed

$$Q'_{oj} = \sqrt{\frac{2C_{oj}A_j}{C_{m_j}(i-2gz)}} \tag{8-4}$$

or

$$Q'_{o_j} = Q_{o_j} \sqrt{\frac{i}{i - 2gz}} \tag{8-5}$$

Definition of capital limitation equation

$$V_{\max} - g \sqrt{\frac{1}{i - 2gz}} \sum_{j=1}^{J} Q_{o_j} C_{m_j} = 0 \tag{8-6}$$

Value of Lagrange multiplier z

$$z = -\frac{i}{2g} \left[\left(\frac{g \sum_{j=1}^{J} Q_{o_j} C_{m_j}}{V_{\max}} \right)^2 - 1 \right] \tag{8-7}$$

Modified economic order quantity reduction factor

$$\sqrt{\frac{i}{i - 2gz}} = \frac{V_{\max}}{g \sum_{j=1}^{J} Q_{o_j} C_{m_j}} \tag{8-8}$$

Unrestricted annual inventory operating cost

$$C = i \sum_{j=1}^{J} Q_{o_j} C_{m_j} \tag{8-9}$$

Restricted inventory operating cost

$$C' = \frac{1}{g} \{(i - gz) V_{\max}\} \tag{8-10}$$

Limit of Lagrange multiplier z

$$-z \leqslant \frac{1}{C_{m_{\max}}} \tag{8-11}$$

Minimum effective value limitation

$$V_{\min} \geqslant \sqrt{\frac{i C_{m_{\max}}}{i C_{m_{\max}} + 2}} \, g \sum_{j=1}^{J} Q_{o_j} C_{m_j} \tag{8-12}$$

Average total storage space value

$$S = g \sum_{=1}^{J} q_j W_j \tag{8-13}$$

Space restriction

$$S_{\max} - g \sum_{j=1}^{J} q_j W_j \geqslant 0 \tag{8-14}$$

Modified economic order quantity when a space limitation is imposed

$$Q''_{o_j} = \sqrt{\frac{2 C_{o_j} A_j}{i C_{m_j} - 2\theta_g W_j}} \tag{8-15}$$

Set-up time restriction

$$T - \sum_{j=1}^{J} \frac{A_j t_j}{q_j} \geqslant 0 \tag{8-16}$$

Annual inventory operating cost

$$C = \sum_{j=1}^{J} \left\{ \frac{C_{oj}A_j}{q_j} + \frac{q_jC_{mj}i}{2} \right\} + \psi \left\{ T - \sum_{j=1}^{J} \frac{A_jt_j}{q_j} \right\} \qquad (8\text{-}17)$$

Modified economic order quantity when a set-up time limitation is imposed

$$Q_{oj}^* = \sqrt{ \left\{ \frac{2A_j(C_{oj} - \psi t_j)}{iC_{mj}} \right\} } \qquad (8\text{-}18)$$

Annual inventory operating cost when a restriction is imposed on both set-up time and invested capital

$$C = \sum_{j=1}^{J} \left\{ \frac{C_{oj}A_j}{q_j} + \frac{q_jC_{mj}i}{2} \right\} + z \left\{ V_{max} - g \sum_{j=1}^{J} q_jC_{mj} \right\}$$
$$+ \psi \left\{ T - \sum_{j=1}^{J} \frac{A_jt_j}{q_j} \right\} \qquad (8\text{-}19)$$

Modified economic order quantity when a restriction is imposed on both set-up time and invested capital

$$q_j = \sqrt{ \left\{ \frac{2A_j(C_{oj} - \psi t_j)}{C_m(i - 2zg)} \right\} } \qquad (8\text{-}20)$$

Modified economic order quantity when a restriction is imposed on both set-up time and storage space

$$q_j = \sqrt{ \left\{ \frac{2A_j(C_{oj} - \psi t_j)}{C_{mj}i - 2\theta g W_j} \right\} } \qquad (8\text{-}21)$$

CHAPTER 9

Average stock level

$$I = \frac{q}{2} + k\sigma_d\sqrt{(R+L)} \qquad (9\text{-}1)$$

Coverage

$$G = \frac{I}{A} = \frac{1}{2m} + \frac{k\sigma_d\sqrt{(R+L)}}{A} \qquad (9\text{-}2)$$

Replenishments per annum per item

$$m_j = Z\sqrt{A_jC_{mj}} \qquad (9\text{-}3)$$

Replenishment order size when replenishments per annum are decided as m_j

$$q_j = \frac{1}{z}\sqrt{\frac{A_j}{C_{mj}}} \qquad (9\text{-}4)$$

14

Appendix B. The Normal Distribution

Standard deviate, k	Customer service level, %	Probability of a stockout occurring, %
1·00	84·1	15·9
1·05	85·3	14·7
1·10	86·4	13·6
1·15	87·5	12·5
1·20	88·5	11·5
1·25	89·4	10·6
1·30	90·0	10·0
1·35	91·2	8·8
1·40	91·9	8·1
1·45	92·7	7·3
1·50	93·3	6·7
1·55	94·0	6·0
1·60	94·5	5·5
1·65	95·1	4·9
1·70	95·5	4·5
1·75	96·0	4·0
1·80	96·4	3·6
1·85	96·8	3·2
1·90	97·1	2·9
1·95	97·4	2·6
2·00	97·7	2·3
2·25	98·8	1·2
2·50	99·4	0·6
2·75	99·7	0·3
3·00	99·9	0·1

Appendix C. The Cumulative Poisson Distribution

CUSTOMER SERVICE LEVEL, %

Re-order level	Average demand during the leadtime								
	2	3	4	5	6	7	8	9	10
2	67·7								
3	85·7	64·7							
4	94·7	81·5	62·9						
5	98·3	91·6	78·5	61·6					
6	99·6	96·7	88·9	76·2	60·6				
7	99·9	98·8	94·9	86·7	74·4	59·9			
8	100·0	99·6	97·9	93·2	84·7	72·9	59·3		
9		99·9	99·2	96·8	91·6	83·1	71·7	58·7	
10		100·0	99·7	98·6	95·7	90·2	81·6	70·6	58·3
11			99·9	99·5	98·0	94·7	88·8	80·3	69·7
12			100·0	99·8	99·1	97·3	93·6	87·6	79·2
13				99·9	99·6	98·7	96·6	92·6	86·5
14				100·0	99·9	99·4	98·2	95·9	91·7
15					100·0	99·8	99·2	97·8	95·1
16						99·9	99·6	98·9	97·3
17						100·0	99·8	99·5	98·6
18							99·9	99·8	99·3
19							100·0	99·9	99·7
20								100·0	99·8
21									99·9
22									100·0

Probability of a stockout occurring, % = 100 − customer service level

Appendix D. The Exponential Distribution

Ratio of re-order level to average demand during the leadtime ($M/\bar{D}.\bar{L}$)	Customer service level, %	Probability of a stockout occurring, %
1·0	63·2	36·8
1·2	69·9	30·1
1·4	75·3	24·7
1·6	79·8	20·2
1·8	83·5	16·5
2·0	86·5	13·5
2·2	88·9	11·1
2·4	90·9	9·1
2·6	92·6	7·4
2·8	93·9	6·1
3·0	95·0	5·0
3·2	95·9	4·1
3·4	96·7	3·3
3·6	97·3	2·7
3·8	97·8	2·2
4·0	98·2	1·8
4·2	98·5	1·5
4·4	98·8	1·2
4·6	99·0	1·0
4·8	99·2	0·8
5·0	99·3	0·7
5·2	99·4	0·6
5·4	99·5	0·5
5·6	99·6	0·4
5·8	99·7	0·3
6·0	99·8	0·2

Index